SOFTWARE CONFIGURATION MANAGEMENT GUIDEBOOK

THE McGRAW-HILL INTERNATIONAL SOFTWARE QUALITY ASSURANCE SERIES

Consulting Editor

Professor D. Ince
The Open University

Other titles in this series

Practical Implementation of Software Metrics	Goodman
Software Testing	Roper
Software Metrics for Product Assessment	Bache and Bazzana
An Introduction to Software Quality Assurance and its implementation	Ince
ISO 9001 and Software Quality Assurance	Ince

Related titles on software engineering are published in an accompanying series: The International Software Engineering Series, also edited by Professor Darrel Ince.

Other professional books by the same author:

The PATRIARCH Series in Software Quality Assurance:

1. The PATRIARCH SQA Handbook
2. The PATRIARCH Manager's SQA Guidebook
3. The PATRIARCH Developer's SQA Guidebook
4. The PATRIARCH Implementer's SQA Guidebook
5. The PATRIARCH Document Quality Assurance and Verification and Validation Handbook
6. The PATRIARCH SQA Planning and Auditing Manual

7. English/Hebrew, Hebrew/English Quality Assurance Dictionary
8. Review and Inspection Manual
9. Software Technical Procedures Manual
10. Software Management Procedures Manual
11. US Department of Defense Std-2167/2168 Companion: An aid and training guide for use of the Military Standard for Mission Critical Software Development
12. DoD Standards 2167/2167A/2168 Auditor's Manual (in a five volume set) for Data Item Descriptions and Procedures

In addition, the author has also written more than 300 professional papers and three books not related to professional subjects.

SOFTWARE CONFIGURATION MANAGEMENT GUIDEBOOK

Mordechai Ben-Menachem

McGRAW-HILL BOOK COMPANY

London · New York · St Louis · San Francisco · Auckland · Bogotá
Caracas · Lisbon · Madrid · Mexico · Milan · Montreal
New Delhi · Panama · Paris · San Juan · São Paulo · Singapore
Sydney · Tokyo · Toronto

Published by
McGRAW-HILL Book Company Europe
Shoppenhangers Road, Maidenhead, Berkshire, SL6 2QL, England
Telephone 0628 23432
Fax 0628 770224

British Library Cataloguing in Publication Data

Ben-Menachem, Mordechai
   Software Configuration Management
   Guidebook. — (McGraw-Hill International
   Software Quality Assurance Series)
   I. Title II. Series
   005.1

   ISBN 0-07-709013-6

Library of Congress Cataloging-in-Publication Data

Ben-Menachem, Mordechai.
   Software configuration management guidebook/Mordechai Ben-Menachem.
     p. cm. — (McGraw-Hill international software quality assurance series)
   Includes index.
   ISBN 0-07-709013-6
   1. Software configuration management. 2. Software configuration management — Case studies.
I. Title. II. Series.
QA76.76.C69B45   1994   94-1102
005.1–dc20   CIP

12345 CL 97654

Typeset by TecSet Ltd, Wallington, Surrey
and printed and bound in Great Britain by Clays Ltd, St Ives plc

To Racheli B.-D. whose smile warms
the winter flower — for continuing
to give, expecting no return, though
(praise G-d) she does not understand.
May she always have a great deal to give.
And to Micky B.-D., for simply being there.

CONTENTS

ACKNOWLEDGEMENTS

I have the pleasure to acknowledge the aid of several people in the development of this book and to use this opportunity to express my thanks. Clearly, the task of writing a book, and perhaps this book in particular, has not been only mine. I am grateful to many people. This brief page can only express thanks to those whose help stood out more than others. The order that my thanks are expressed is strictly chronological and should not be construed in any other manner.

Firstly, I must begin by thanking Dr Garry Marliss who took the trouble to review the initial draft of this book, indeed long before it could really be called a book. The help provided by the excellent comments, both personal and professional, made this task very significantly simpler and clearer.

Secondly, I have the great pleasure to express my thanks to my editor Ms Jackie Harbor of McGraw-Hill in Maidenhead, England. It would be superfluous to say that this would not have been possible without her help and patience. She has been also an encouragement. I am certain that her efforts will be properly rewarded.

Finally, I can express my thanks to the reviewers of this book. While it is certainly true that they did a job for McGraw-Hill, the quality of their comments and suggestions allowed this book to be completed.

INTRODUCTION

GENESIS

In the beginning of the 'software revolution', towards the end of the 1970s, there grew to be an increasing awareness that software is very different from hardware — but also possesses many striking similarities. Interestingly, this new awareness grew both in the professional community and in the management of their organizations. One of the things that became noticeable was that many of these similarities could be utilized to decrease some of the degrees of uncertainty that were inherent in the process of creating software and software-rich projects.

For one thing, it was becoming obvious that a greater percentage of budgets was being devoted to software (as opposed to hardware) and that the problems with systems were usually more directly related to the software than the hardware. As a matter of fact, and this is rather shocking, as the percentage of the software in a product increased, the percentage of the errors from software increased — at a faster rate. These trends (and others) caused a great deal of fear. One of the symptoms of this fear was the, now famous, Ada project, the basic approach being to apply *some* sort of discipline to the software process.

One of the results of this process was an enhanced awareness that software, and software professionals, *can be managed*! This was actually quite a revelation. It took us — the professional community — more or less until the mid-1980s to discover this seeming triviality. What happened directly as a result of this was a plethora of 'structured' techniques — sometimes *ad nauseam*. These were always presented as the newest and best panacea. This has still not proven to be the case. As it turns out, the greatest boon to developing good software and releasing it on time and within budget is what has always worked best in every human endeavour — courageous men and women doing their job in the best way they know how and managing their endeavours conscientiously.

In the final analysis, what we learned is that good software demands a large amount of hard work coupled with an equal amount of 'total dedication'. We also learned that this hard work can be accomplished better if we learn from other areas of technology which have garnered more experience. In terms of the management of the job, probably the most striking aspect which we have adapted from other engineering disciplines is that discipline known as 'Configuration Management'.

This book is designed as a guidebook for the software practitioner. The professionals being addressed are those who have recognized a need for the application of Software Configuration Management (SCM) in the projects with which he or she is involved. This book is a beginner's guide to SCM. It is intended for the beginner in Configuration Management (not software development or management). The fact that someone is a 'beginner' in SCM does not mean that there is any lack of management expertise. In this sense, SCM is like any management task. Be aware of concepts which can help make a manager exceptional. They affect SCM just like anything else.

Trust your subordinates. Do not expect them to go all out for you if they are not convinced that you believe in them and in what they are doing. People want to follow someone who knows where he or she is going. Know when to be an expert. From boardroom to mailroom, everyone had better understand that if you say something, it is because you can show that you know what you're talking about. There is nothing wrong with not knowing. Just do not make efforts to advertise the fact. Invite dissent. Your people aren't giving you their best or learning how to lead if they are afraid to speak up. Simplify. You need to see the big picture in order to set a course, communicate it, and maintain it. Keep the details at bay.

OUR EXPECTATIONS

It is expected that the reader of this book has at least a working knowledge of software development, and preferably also some knowledge, or predilection for, software management. This working knowledge should have been gained as the result of experience (as opposed to an 'academic' knowledge). This may be either as a developer or as an experienced user or manager. No other expertise is expected.

To put it another, much lighter way, there is a good joke I heard somewhere (I apologize for not being able to cite the source: I do not know it).

> There was a party with a large group of highly educated professionals of many types. During the course of the evening, a discussion ensued as to what actually was the 'oldest profession'(!). As the discussion progressed one very well known lady stood up and said: 'All you male chauvinists claiming that soldiering is an old profession, you all know what the oldest profession was . . .' Her inference was, of course, quite clear to any cultured individual. It was certainly not needed for her to continue.
>
> As the merits of this case were being debated, a doctor stood up and addressed the lady in question: 'Now madam, you don't really think such a complicated operation as the removal of a rib could have been accomplished (not to mention the second part) without a doctor being present?' This also was a good case. And the issue would certainly have been decided had not a programmer suddenly become frustrated and shouted: '. . . and who do you think created the Chaos . . .?!!!' This argument won the day.
>
> If the author of this can be found, I shall be only too happy to give credit.

Unfortunately, it may simply be true. The real story of this book is Controlling Chaos. That is an oxymoron of no mean proportion.

THE STRUCTURE OF THE BOOK

This book is designed to serve the software developer as a tool for accomplishing a specific task. While it is not a 'cookbook', it is intended to allow fast and convenient implementation of Software Configuration Management. As such, the book includes specific subsections to help the practitioner expedite task implementation.

The task of evaluation, for instance, part of any implementation process, must certainly include checklists for the evaluation of the Software Configuration Management process as performed by the installation (or project). Evaluations of this sort may be performed for either or both of two purposes:

1. That of auditing to ensure the proper procedures are being carried out at a contractor's or subcontractor's installation.
2. Initiating the process of Software Configuration Management at an installation which has not previously had experience with this discipline.

The major problem to be addressed in both of these cases is a swift and accurate collection of data (as much data as possible) which reflects how the process is being performed. In most cases, there is a process of some kind for Software Configuration Management. The process may not be particularly sophisticated, and perhaps not be computerized — it does not always need to be so. Well thought out manual systems can frequently be quite adequate.

In addition to the actual questions of the checklists there are also a few forms to aid in the evaluation process (see Appendix 5).

CASE STUDIES

Another type of item added to the book for the purpose of assisting the practitioner is a series of case studies. This book includes several kinds of case study, as detailed below. These can be used by the reader to gain a better understanding of the applicability of a specific aspect to his or her own situation.

There are three types of case study:

1. There are case studies embedded unassumingly, as part of various chapters, which are intended to lightly focus some light upon a specific aspect of a process.
2. There are larger case studies, discussed and presented separately as within the text. These present the reader with a broad discussion of a problem, with specific relevance to an item of the whole project.
3. Finally, there are two major case studies, presented as separate chapters, to illustrate Software Configuration Management Plans. These are numbered as Chapters 12 and 13, and are placed directly after the spot in the text devoted to these plans. Some words of guidance in the use of these chapters:

   (a) Those who are in need of producing software according to the directives of the United States Department of Defense will probably want to read both of these chapters. The first will supply them with the information concerning the writing of a DoD approved plan. The second chapter will supply the reader with additional information, particularly concerning critical projects.

(b) Those who are involved in non-military projects can probably omit the chapter concerning the DoD projects. The information there will, in most cases, not be needed by them. Possible exceptions will be those projects which are highly critical or exceedingly difficult.

GUIDEBOOK DESIGN CONCEPTS

This book is designed to benefit all those projects which are too large to be able to handle, in an effective manner, the quantities of items in the project. That usually means several tens of files and/or involvement of too many people for the communications between them to be trivial (this usually means more than three). This book is not intended to solve the Configuration Management problems of large complicated military projects — though it can certainly help them. There is a basic need to simply get started! This is by no means an easy thing to do. Many projects, staffed by first-rate professionals, simply have no idea how to begin the subject of Configuration Management. For one thing, it is still not taught in most universities, especially not as part of the computer science curriculum. Viewing the development of the computer milieu, it is obvious that an increased emphasis upon optimization of management techniques could potentially benefit the majority of projects.

Software Configuration Management is the most effective management and communication tool in existence for truly understanding and following processes which occur during the evolution of a product or system. In the systems being created today, there is an imploring need to follow the patterns of changes which occur in requirements, data, designs, code, documentation and other items. Increasingly, both developers and users are demanding that they are using the correct data for what they are doing. With the increase in computing power has come an increase in the quantities of data. We must not, of course, lose sight of the realities: many projects are quite successful and are supplied on time and within budget — these products meet their requirements and are delivered at the cost expected. This book intends to make that job easier and less expensive. Unfortunately, many projects go quite wrong! Deliveries are late and with only partial functionality — with frequent budget overruns measured in hundreds of per cent. This is, of course, more true for those systems (products) which are software rich than for those which are based upon older, more disciplined, technologies.

In utilizing the tools of Software Configuration Management, we can more easily know what we are supposed to build, what we are building and what we have built. That does not mean we cannot use Software Configuration Management incorrectly. (Remember the old rule of the systems analyst: 'Computerizing a sloppy factory makes for computerized slop!') With almost no effort, anything can be made to go wrong. This has been known for a long time. In fact, 'Murphy's Law' predates Murphy by about 2000 years. The first such 'law' appears in the Bible, in the book of Amos!

However, the tools of Software Configuration Management, when implemented intelligently and with proper forethought, can serve as the focal point for a real discipline, at a very low cost to the project. This means that not only can we know what has happened, we can support the product effectively. We can repeat the good things we have done and learn from them.

Let us take a moment to examine some of the cost/benefits of Software Configuration Management (SCM):

- Many people think that the penalties which Software Configuration Management entails outweigh the benefits. Clearly, a system like this does have a cost. However, in direct money terms, SCM consistently saves money.
- Certainly, starting SCM on a very large project at a late date is more difficult than beginning the project with the discipline interwoven into it from the start. However, the benefits to be gained from SCM, even at a late date, are well worth the effort. The speed and facility of generating quality documentation, using appropriate tools, improves the internal communications of the project to an extent that no other method can. Far from stultifying engineering creativity, we find that the proper application of this discipline frees the engineers from onerous duties, which they neither enjoy nor wish to perform.
- Finally, it has been stated that the imposition of procedures creates time delays and extra work. This can be both true and false. Many benefits accrue when the total accessibility (and 'assess' ability) of changes can be assured. A well-designed SCM system, with emphasis upon getting the work done in a disciplined manner, prevents many, many more problems than it can possibly create.

LIST OF ABBREVIATIONS

The following abbreviations are likely to turn up when looking at questions relating to Configuration Management. Though this list is far from exhaustive, it attempts to include most of the abbreviations relating to both Hardware Configuration Management and Software Configuration Management. However, for those who actually wish to **communicate**, we recommend using these abbreviations sparingly.

AB/L	Allocated baseline
BoM	Bill of 'materials'
CA	Configuration audit
CC	Configuration control
CCB	Change Control Board
CDR	Critical design review
CI	Configuration identification
CM	Configuration Management
CPCI	Computer program configuration item (DoD-STD-2167)
CSC	Computer software component (DoD-Std-2167/2167A)
CSCI	Computer software configuration item (DoD-Std-2167A)
ECP	Engineering change proposal
FB/L	Functional baseline
FCA	Functional configuration audit
GFE	Government furnished equipment
ICB	Interface Control Board
ICWG	Interface Control Working Group
MGMT	Management
ODC	Other direct cost
O&M	Operation and maintenance
PB/L	Product baseline

PCA	Physical configuration audit
PCI	Product configuration audit
PCR	Program change report
PDR	Preliminary design review
PTR	Program trouble report
QA	Quality assurance
RDW	Request for deviation/waiver
R&M	Reliability and maintainability
SCCB	Software Change Control Board
SCCS	Source Code Control System
SCM	Software Configuration Management
SCMP	Software Configuration Management Plan
SDR	Software design review
Spec	Specification
SRR	System requirements review
UDF	Unit development folder
VDD	Version description document
WBS	Work breakdown structure

The Quality Forum is pleased to publish jointly with McGraw-Hill this book which covers topics pertinent to software quality assurance.

The aim of the organization is 'to help the member organizations improve the quality of their products and services through the exchange of information between members and with other organizations with similar interests'.

The Quality Forum has over 200 members, including organizations from all sectors of industry and commerce, as well as local and national government. While these organizations are predominantly based in the UK, this includes a growing number from other countries in Europe.

This series of books aims to provide an opportunity for authors to publish works which are both practical and state-of-the-art. In this way Quality Forum members and other organizations will benefit from the exchange of information and the development of new ideas which will further the cause of quality in Information Technology.

The Quality Forum publishes these books with the aim of stimulating discussion in the software community so that the industry as a whole will move forward to improved products and services. It is proud to be associated with the series while not endorsing every single point of view in every book.

If you would like to know more about the Quality Forum, please contact:

Quality Forum
17 St Catherine's Rd
Ruislip
Middlesex HA4 7RX
UK
Tel: +44 (0) 895 635222
Fax: +44 (0) 895 679178

1

THE CONCEPT OF CONFIGURATION MANAGEMENT

FROM THE LITERATURE

Quite a large amount of material has been published in the professional literature about Software Configuration Management. In the Additional Reading and Standards sections of this book (Appendices 2 and 3) are listed seventeen books, twelve articles, fourteen reports, twenty-four 'major' military standards and forty-one 'sub-standards' (and these only from the United States Department of Defense), three standards produced by the Institute of Electrical and Electronic Engineers (IEEE) and one standard from the International Standards Organization (ISO). There is also a table which shows the existence of others. By no means does this list pretend to be exhaustive — though it is fairly representative. The problem with most of the books that have been written is that they are not really intended for the practitioner with the immediate need to implement Software Configuration Management within their projects.

Babich (1986, p. 8; see Appendix 2) has stated the following:

> On any team project, a certain degree of confusion is inevitable. The goal is to minimize the confusion so that more work can get done. The art of coordinating software development to minimize this particular type of confusion is called Configuration Management. Configuration Management is the art of identifying, organizing and controlling modifications to the software being built by a programming team. The goal is to maximize productivity by minimizing mistakes.

This definition is rather droll. Certain aspects of it can be significantly improved. Let us begin by using an 'official' definition. The *IEEE Standard Glossary of Software Engineering Terminology* (the version approved on 15 February 1991) defines Configuration Management as:

> A discipline applying technical and administrative direction and surveillance to: identify and document the functional and physical characteristics of a configuration item, control changes to those characteristics, record and report change processing and implementation status, and verify compliance with specified requirements.

1

Clearly, this definition provides a great deal more information. Firstly, one can see that Configuration Management is a discipline. A discipline is not readily defined as an art form — which tends to imply a much greater degree of freedom than we should properly want for the proper engineering of technical products. Secondly, mere identification of what is (and has been) happening is not sufficient. The objective must be to identify and document; and this process must include both the conceptual and the physical aspects of the system. These points are very important. In later chapters we shall see that this has a profound effect upon the Configuration Management Plan. Thirdly, controlling of changes must include all the aspects of the product, whether they are conceptual (such as those reflected by a requirement's definition document), physical or simply directional (management directives of any sort). Also, these controls must record and provide reporting facilities for everyone who deals in changes for any development object which can change. Lastly, the discipline must facilitate a process of verification and compliance. This may take the form of certain types of reports or a 'methodology' (apologies for the use of this over-used word, but it does sometimes apply).

Certainly, we could expand upon this and include other, alternative, definitions, such as those in the United States Department of Defense standards (DoD-Std-480A and MIL-Std-483A, and others) but in the interests of brevity, and real information, this is not really productive. It is unlikely that other definitions would significantly increase our understanding at this point.

OUR WORKING DEFINITION

Generally, our working definition of Configuration Management, for the purposes of this book, includes six points. They are as follows:

1. A **Management** discipline which
2. **Identifies** the proposed or implemented (actual) configuration of a system
3. At discrete points in **time**
4. Systematically **records and traces** changes to all system components (conceptual and physical)
5. Provides tools for **control**ling changes; and finally
6. Allows everything happening with (and to) the system, throughout the **entire life-cycle** of the system, to be **verified** via auditing and reporting tools

All this is expressly for purposes of assuring: integrity, accountability, visibility, reproducibility, project coordination and traceability and formal control of system/product evolution. Configuration Management (in the context of this book) is a process used for more efficiently developing and maintaining software. This is accomplished by improving: accountability, reproducibility, traceability and coordination.

BUT, *WHAT* EXACTLY ARE WE TALKING ABOUT?

A configuration is a list of parts, and their relative arrangement. This includes the number, nature and interconnections of all constituent parts. The configuration of our system is the exact (well defined) list of all parts used, their relative arrangement and the methods to be used to construct our system from these parts.

However, this book is not simply about Configuration Management, but about Software Configuration Management. Software is:

- Structured information with hierarchical, logical and functional properties
- Created as text but maintained in several, and frequently parallel, representations during the life-cycle of the product
- Machine 'processable' in its most advanced state
- Maintained in various forms, and with different tools, during development, use, maintenance and operations
- Composed of parts which are themselves software
- Created via the use of tools, which are themselves also software

The nature of the 'soft . . .' in software is a very significant aspect. For one thing, it may mean that it cannot readily be understood by people whose previous experiences have taught them to understand things which are completely 'hard.' — meaning concrete, tangible. For another, 'soft' also means that everything is very 'fluid' and may be easy to change. This can be very good (which is why software is so common) but can also be very dangerous — which is why software production, as a discipline, has a history of about fifty per cent failures (in terms of projects). These are the reasons that change needs to be tightly controlled. Therefore: a software configuration is a well defined arrangement of software parts and the *exact* procedure(s) and tools to be used for (re)constructing the product or system from (or with) these parts. This *must* also include procedures for reconstructing various (e.g. previous) versions or releases.

Software Configuration Management addresses three of the most critical problems facing any development and/or maintenance project involving multiple developers. These are the problems of *shared data*, *double maintenance* and *simultaneous updates*.

Since the concept of system life-cycle has been mentioned several times, it should be defined and put into context. A system life-cycle is a sequence of stages — more or less formally defined — through which a system evolves. This begins from definition of the earliest conceptual need and passes through to the final retirement of the system (replacement of the system by its successor). Enormous amounts of literature have been written about this subject, and a discussion of it is certainly not part of the scope of this book. Readers interested in this subject should refer to one of the standard texts on software engineering for a further explanation. There is also an IEEE standard that may be of interest.

OF WHAT IS SCM COMPOSED?

Software Configuration Management (SCM), as we have defined it, is a discipline. As with any discipline, it can be rigidly analysed into its constituent parts. The discipline of SCM is composed of exactly four activities or parts: **Identification**; **Control**; **Status Accounting** and **Auditing**. At the risk of getting slightly ahead of ourselves, but to avoid confusion, some very brief explanation may be in order:

- **Identification** refers to the general structure of the product being produced and how the items are to be identified.
- **Control** refers to the methods to be implemented for the management and technical control of the myriad configuration items identified.
- **Status Accounting** refers to reporting to all concerned — management, client and technical — information describing items and their status.
- **Auditing** refers to activities which are designed the assure the correct functioning of the SCM system, as defined.

This particular breakdown has been accepted as an industry standard. Firstly, it was accepted by the IEEE as document IEEE Std-828-1990 on 28 September 1990 (this is the latest version; the full history of previous versions is outside the scope of this book — we shall just mention that this particular document is an update of IEEE Std-828-1983). This standard was later accepted by the American National Standards Institute on 15 February 1991.

In the terminology used by the IEEE set of standards, and as recommended by this book, these four SCM parts are defined and described by individual sections of the Software Configuration Management Plan. These parts, their abbreviations and the section of the IEEE standard (Std-828-1990) that describes the activity are defined in Table 1.1. In addition, corresponding sections of a Software Configuration Management Plan are also defined in Table 1.1. Note that this is a format recommended by this author's accumulated experience. It is the format that has been defined by the previous version of IEEE Std-828 (from 1983). The present version of 828 declines to support a specific format for the plan document but defines a different structure of information. This structure has frequently been found to be 'over-kill' for the majority of projects. However, if the project which needs to be planned is very complex and large, by all means please refer to the standard (ANSI/IEEE Std-828-1990).

Table 1.1 SCM activities

SCM activity or part	Abbreviaton	Defined by section of 828	Suggested section in the SCM Plan
Identification	SCI	2.3.1	2
Control	SCC	2.3.2	3
Status Accounting	SCSA	2.3.3	4
Audits and Reviews	SCA	2.3.4	5

In addition, it may be useful to 'map' this structure of activities, described by the plan, to the classes of information with which a Software Configuration Management Plan must be concerned. ANSI/IEEE Std-828-1990 describes six classes of information (Table 1.2). Each class describes a certain idea and maps with corresponding activities.

'Introduction' refers to the general structure of the document (purpose, scope, references, etc.). 'Management' refers to the way the activities concerned with are to be managed and by whom. This, of course, includes a description of their responsibilities, with all that that may imply.

Table 1.2   SCM information

Information class	Defined by Section of 828	Section in the SCM Plan
Introduction	2.1	1
Management	2.2	2
Activities	2.3	3
Schedules	2.4	4
Resources	2.5	5
Plan Maintenance	2.6	6

'Activities' refers, essentially, to all those activities described in Table 1.1. This, by the way, is a primary reason for the degrees of complexity which the new version of the standard causes. All these activities are 'squashed' (unrealistically) into one section which then becomes quite large.

'Schedules' refers to when specific actions or activities must occur, in relation to other development tasks. Hopefully, the SCM Plan should live for as long as the product is still 'alive'. Hence, this section is quite small. Everything happens, all the time, forever (this is, of course, a bit of an exaggeration).

'Resources' refers to a description of the tools and human resources to be used for the SCM tasks. Finally, 'Plan Maintenance' refers to the methods to be used to ensure that the SCM Plan itself remains a valuable document. From experience, the best way to ensure this is for the SCM system to be so good that everyone wants it!

In the following sections we deal primarily with the four activities listed in Table 1.1 and with other aspects of the process that are relevant to the real-life implementation of the discipline in an organization or project. These other aspects include, for instance, the tools to be used for the implementation and the methods to be used for planning SCM. Each section dealing with a specific activity begins with the relevant definition of the activity — taken from the previously quoted IEEE Standard.

In any case, it must be noted that currently a significant amount of software development is performed in a distributed environment. As such, the reader must bear in mind that all Software Configuration Management *must* accommodate Distributed Configuration Management or risk being made irrelevant by the realities of the development environments.

Checklist 1.1 can be used for evaluating the **scope** of the system under consideration for the preparation of an SCMP. Specifically, this checklist aids the analyst in defining the **identification** and **purpose** of the system — the major portions of the scope.

In terms of checklist usage, the reader should note that all of the checklists in this book are structured having the intention of affirmative answers. That is, the assumption is that if all questions can be answered 'yes', then the analyst has used this information breakdown 'correctly'.

Checklist 1.1   Evaluating the scope of the system

Identification and purpose of the system

- Are the boundaries of the system to be audited clearly delineated?
- Have these definitions been made a part of the system's specifications?

- Has the purpose of the system and the function of the computers been clearly defined?
- Have the criteria for system requirements allocations to the various configuration items been clearly established and made public?
- Is the Configuration Management system to be audited clearly defined?
- Have all tools to be used for the management of the system's configurations been put into place, or has a clear schedule been allocated for such?
- Does an organization exist for the performance of the Configuration Management duties?
- Are the Configuration Management audits defined publicly?

PERSONNEL

As in any management discipline, and particularly a discipline that is frequently only partially understood (even by many first-rate professionals), it is critical here to question *who* is to perform the task. Characteristics of personnel needed for efficient performance of Software Configuration Management tasks must be paid close attention to. This section describes some of this information in an introductory and summary manner. More of this subject will be discussed, in much greater detail, later on in the book.

In principle, there are five information items concerning 'peopling-up' that must be examined in detail. Remember that, at this point, the discussion concerns the initial planning (the scope of the plan) not the fine details:

1. The **number** of personnel needed for each software configuration management task — this will be needed for project budgeting. Our usual rule of thumb is that, once the system has been set up, we should need one person per project group, for about five per cent of their professional time.
2. The expected **skill levels** for all those involved. The professional to set the system up must be at a very high skill level. The person to run the system (as referred to in 1) can be at a much lower level.
3. The job **titles** of those to perform the tasks are significant — as are the 'teeth' attached to their jobs, allowing them to make certain things happen.
4. Geographic **location**s — are all the people local, at the site, or are some of them located at a remote site?
5. Are any special **security** clearances needed? This does not only refer to 'military' kinds of security! Many (most) commercial enterprises have security issues to deal with. Certainly, all organizations must, at very least, have backups to prevent loss in case of hardware failure.

2

SOFTWARE CONFIGURATION IDENTIFICATION

TO BEGIN THE PROCESS . . .

As stated, we shall begin this section with a formal definition as taken from the IEEE standard (ANSI/IEEE 610.12-1991). The standard contains two definitions, but only the first of them is relevant here. Configuration Identification is described as follows:

> (1) An element of configuration management, consisting of selecting the configuration items for a system and recording their functional and physical characteristics in technical documentation.

What is this referring to, in the terms needed to be applied to our project? The process of selecting the configuration items is not quite as simple as it may seem. It is not merely a process of identifying that the system has (say) 50, or 500, files. This may be sufficient for small systems consisting of up to (say) 100 files. The degree of complexity involved in a system of these proportions can be readily handled, particularly with the aid of a computerized configuration manager (in this sense, the Configuration Management software is acting the role of a 'simple' librarian). It begins to become more complex when the system is large (several thousand files) and/or the interrelations between the files are complex.

A ready example might be a system which is composed of (say) four subsystems, each of which is composed of several modules, each module being composed of several code units, which in turn also have several 'include' files, all these contained in individual files. Also, there is a common set of 'library' routines which everyone uses. In addition to this, we must maintain:

- Documentation
- The specifications and designs
- The test designs, data and reports
- The change and problem reports

- The 'make' files which direct and document the way the system is constructed (these may sometimes be called 'build' files), etc.

This is a very small example of how the level of complexity rises, even for as small a system as this example implies, due to both the quantities of individual items to be created and maintained and the complexities of their interrelationships.

In this type of situation, which is actually the common case, it is not only a question of simply 'selecting' the items, but rather of deciding upon a general method for the process of selecting. This concept of a generalized method for identification is referred to as the system 'granularity'. This implies the 'size of the grains' of which the system is composed. These become the pieces that we are going to want to manage with our Configuration Management system/process.

Thus, the rules governing the process of software configuration identification (SCI) are:

1. SCI defines the 'granularity' of the SCM.
2. SCI then defines what is needed to be seen (i.e. what needs to be visible) by all those who will have to see what is happening on the project. This does not mean only those who need access to the project's files: it may also mean (say) client staff who need to receive information which is processed from these files.
3. SCI ensures that the identification scheme selected reflects the structure of the product, the project and the organization.
4. The identification process must always be coupled with a parallel process of labelling the item with a distinct and unique label.
5. Note that the size of the 'grains' identified by the SCI process can never be consistent (more on this conundrum, below).
6. SCI is a critical project management task.

However, we have only discussed here the rules governing the process. We have not yet discussed the criteria for the actual selection. The section (below, after the example items) discussing identification principles deals with this issue.

EXAMPLES OF ITEMS TO BE IDENTIFIED

Of course, none of this can be particularly understandable without some concrete examples. Software parts come in as many forms as does software. Each different type of part may need a different concept of handling. The handling methods may depend upon size and connectivity to other parts, as well. Software parts will typically be (this is, of course, only a partial list):

- Requirements specifications
- Design/interface specifications
- Test designs/test data
- Programs/procedures/source code
- Files
- Object code
- EPROMs

- Media
- Command files/make files
- Software tools
- Software Quality Assurance Plan
- Software Configuration Management Plan
- Software Verification and Validation Plan
- User documentation

Alternatively, software parts might be: a variable; individual keystrokes; a single line in a COBOL program — any identifiable item. These, of course, are too small to be generally relevant. To manage a product from such tiny items would probably doom any project to failure. For our purposes, a software part is the 'smallest piece' of software which you are going to want to manage. And here is that little conundrum mentioned previously. We always wish to manage the system as a whole — as a single item. But, of course, all systems consist of constituent parts, which may themselves exist at several levels (files, modules, subsystems, . . .). The granularity of a system can never be consistent. This aspect frequently causes a great deal of confusion, unless carefully considered in advance. One other point: notice that this discussion is not limited to the software parts of the system. The documentation and the media are of no less importance. See the checklist below which is devoted exclusively to these aspects.

IMPORTANT IDENTIFICATION PRINCIPLES

Now that we have gained a basic understanding of the concepts behind configuration identification, we can examine the exact principles and criteria which need to govern our process of identification of software items. First, we present the principles according to the way they must be applied. There are six principles, in three categories. Afterwards, below, we shall discuss the criteria for the selection of the items. We must define the following:

- How are the items labelled?
- Who does it?

Finally, we must understand the concept of baselines and decide what do we do with them.

LABELS:
1. *Software items are labelled at discrete points in time.* In a computerized environment, a date/time stamp is quite natural. In a process of labelling items, the date/time stamp is absolutely essential. The second principle expands upon this.
2. *Each item's label is related to labels of predecessors and siblings.* This relationship must be made very obvious. It can be via a numbers/mnemonics hierarchy. For instance, an item labelled '2.3' clearly is later than something labelled '2.1' and earlier than '2.5'. This number is used here for illustrative purposes and is only part of the label. The label will usually consist of two parts, a name and a revision (or version) number. The number is the time-related part, as it changes over time with each instance of the particular part being revised. The name must remain constant over time for this item.

Finally, particularly for embedded software (e.g. [EP]ROMs) the media need to be linked with software and 'versioned'.

THE ORGANIZATIONAL RESPONSIBILITY:
3. *One organization performs labelling throughout the project/product life-cycle.* In a technological environment, every item has a discernible life-cycle, a beginning and an end. An organization needs to be delegated and made responsible for all activities concerning the labelling of items. That includes all project titling, labelling and numbering. If there is a possibility of duplicate item names, it generally results in chaos. Even more so, if one detects something like that occurring (i.e. a lack of clear authority for the item labelling process) this is usually a sign that something is *very* wrong with the project.

BASELINING:
4. *Partitioning a baseline is always subjective.* So far we have discussed individual items. However, as mentioned above, there are also items which are aggregates of items. The topmost aggregate item is the product or system. Any time this item (i.e. the system) is 'released' this is called a *baseline*. More on this, with a formal definition, appears below. The actual partitioning of the baseline into its constituent parts is subjective — and is even frequently the subject of quite heated debates. There are no ironclad rules for this, nor can there be.
5. *Create some partition and maintain it.* Whatever partition is decided upon, *remember* that once you have created a partitioning of the baseline, redoing it can be an enormous job. This is an early decision which must be made and must be 'correct' from the beginning! This implies that almost any amount of debate — at the time the partitioning process is performed — and review is well worth the time spent.
6. *Baselines live forever.* Once a baseline is created–defined–released, it (the baseline) can never change! If a change is made, it is a new baseline.

There is always a difficulty, even with these principles, of exactly which items should then be configuration items and which should be more-or-less hidden — 'Hidden' meaning that they are never really managed as separate entities (for example, an individual chapter of the user manual). The actual selection is a management decision, albeit a low-level one. The decision-making is based upon the system engineering process and upon engineering and logistics. The emphasis upon system engineering is significant because, in any case, the process must be based upon experience, knowledge of the principles and their implications, an understanding of the project and technical considerations. In any case, this will all be based upon inherent system characteristics and interface requirements. In addition, this will always be influenced by our need to control and consideration of the customer's needs (for a project: if it is a product development then think of the marketing people).

The four general criteria which are recommended to be used for the selection of the actual items are the following (their order is random and has no significance):

1. Certainly, every individual operational program, including utilities and diagnostic programs, and those which are not truly directly related to others. ('Unrelated' might be a training program.)

2. Even more so, everything which has the potential for multiple use, in other projects or systems. (Hopefully, for the sake of your costs, this will be a very broad category.)
3. The capabilities of the functions developed, particularly those which may be delivered at different times (in other words, expect to take into account the development schedule).
4. Items which are of a particularly volatile nature, such as those with a particularly high technical importance or having separate, detailed specifications.

IDENTIFY PROJECT BASELINES

Baselines integrate groups together. We must of course remember that the software is created by people: people who are by their nature individualists. The recognition of a summation of their work (to date) by declaring a baseline is a recognition that they have completed a stage of the project. This is very good for the overall morale of the project.

Each 'Build' and each software library within the project, as well as each release (major or minor), is, and has, an individual baseline.

The baselining process also describes the construction of the aggregates. That is to say, *how* the aggregate must be constructed, be put together. This is not a trivial problem. We must know:

- Which tools need to be utilized
- Which parts are connected and which are not
- What are the natures of the interconnections

Once an item is tied into a baseline, changes are made only via a formalized process. This process is usually called the CCB — the Change Control Board. See Chapter 5 on Configuration Control for the details about this.

What all this leads to is a basic statement of what baselines are and why they are important: baselines define the state of the system at a given point in time. The proper recording of this information can be absolutely critical for the success of any project!

Finally, let us examine the formal, IEEE definitions of the concept of baseline:

(1) A specification or product that has been formally reviewed and agreed upon, that thereafter serves as the basis for further development, and that can be changed only through formal procedures.
(2) A document or set of such documents formally designated and fixed at a specific time during the life cycle of a configuration item.

REVISION/VERSION IDENTIFICATION

The difference between revisions and versions is a frequent source of confusion. Let us examine the twin concepts to gain an understanding of where they are similar and where they differ. To begin with, it is worth noting that this discussion refers to the numeric part of the label. (The name should not suffer from the same schizophrenia.) Originally, revisions referred to individual items while versions referred to aggregates. However, this has occasionally been found to be insufficient. What has become prevalent lately is that the revision refers to items that are 'internal' (to the developing organization) while the version refers to released products. This then solves the rather cross-eyed linkage between versions and aggregates. Numbers usually start at 1.0. Sometimes marketing people try to gain an advantage over the competition by artificially beginning with a higher number. This is not part of good management, it is a salesman's ploy. (It is also slightly dishonest!) The following numbers are automatically computed by the SCM system. This automatic computation can be manually overridden, within reason. 'Branch' revisions also need to be identified (e.g. 1.2.3.4). A branch is an agreed-upon split of an item into multiple iterations.

What are the purposes of this? Let us list them: it identifies an instance of the item, product or system; it provides for project milestones; the software life-cycle is performed more 'naturally' by the use of levels; it provides an exact and unique mapping between a version label and module revisions (a version is linked to a specific instance of a revision); a revision may have many version labels.

VISIBILITY AND TRACEABILITY

Finally, there are two terms frequently used to illustrate the power and usefulness of these concepts. They are 'visibility' and 'traceability'. Visibility means permitting the software to be seen by anyone who is allowed to see it: permitting management to 'see' what is happening and permitting management to be seen on a project; that is, permitting them to really manage. Traceability is the ability to link individual events and parts to each other, in time. Remember! All parts have events — all events have parts! In other words, the basic point to all this is that it allows the project to be well managed.

CONFIGURATION IDENTIFICATION NUMBERING

For purposes of identification of items, a system of configuration identification numbers is both most common and most convenient. In some cases (e.g. large, complex, military systems) this can be very complex. However, in most cases, the numbering system should be kept simple. Typically, a numbering system for identifying the revisions of each item, accompanied by a mnemonic, is sufficient.

The most common method is the following:

- The version/revision number consists of two parts, separated by a dot (a period).
- The first part (that is, the part to the *right* of the dot) denotes the current revision from the last baseline.
- The second part (to the *left* of the dot) denotes the number of the last baseline.
- Generally, the right-hand number will be zeroed with each baseline.

Case study 2.1 points out what the effects of Software Configuration Management can mean to a developing system. This particular incident proved to this author the overall value of this technology for allowing a job to be accomplished. Actually, if the reader has come this far, perhaps *convincing* is not what is needed. However, even if the reader does not feel a need for it (I think he or she is probably wrong) it will certainly be useful to show to management for ensuring (enhancing) their support.

Case study 2.1

Some years ago, an excellent professional that I know was responsible for a very large project in the area of telephony (about 300 staff-years of effort in software). As I was responsible for the software quality assurance of the subproject building the control software for the system, he related to me the following case story.

The project was performed in several locations internationally, in parallel. One part of the project — the switch — was being developed by a very large and well respected firm in the United States. This part of the project got stuck! They had reached a release number which can only be described as bordering upon the absurd: something like '84' is the number I recall being quoted to me. Despite this enormous amount of work, the system was still not functional.

When this manager arrived, a total suspension of all work was implemented. Before any more work would be invested, he ordered the immediate implementation of a Software Configuration Management system (there was no organized tracking beforehand). They chose to implement a computerized SCM system, implemented on their mainframe computer. As far as I recall, the system used was an in-house development. Though it was never marketed as a product (unfortunate, it was quite advanced for its time) I shall refrain from referring to it by name. This untied the knot!

With the implementation of this management tool, which the developing company had viewed as being simply a method of recording history, the system suddenly began to work, and quite satisfactorily.

Checklists 2.1–2.5 now follow. This author recommends that the practitioner use them for software configuration identification — the first of the four tasks which must be addressed by the plan. The checklists are functionally divided into the various subtasks for which identification must be made. Once again, the intention is that the questions be answered in the affirmative.

Checklist 2.1

Configuration identification

- Nomenclature, documentation, media, configuration items and revision/version identities

Nomenclature

- Have project nomenclature and standards been defined for the system and can they be easily referenced?
- Has 'ownership' been established for the nomenclature to be used?
- Has a project-wide 'dictionary of terms' been established and made generally available?

- Have these procedures been published and made public knowledge?
- Are all procedures defined in a manner which is readily auditable?
- Have these procedures been implemented?
- Have methods been established to identify every internal development configuration?
- Have methods to be used for the definition and establishment of development configurations been described?

Identification methods

- Have all methods to be used for the identification of configuration items been detailed?
- Do these methods include those techniques for identifying baselined and revised:
  - (a) Subsystems (CSCIs)?
  - (b) Modules (CSCs)?
  - (c) Software units (CSUs)?
  - (d) Technical documents?
  - (e) Managerial documents (e.g. formal plans)?
  - (f) Memos and technical briefs?
  - (g) Non-deliverable software items?
  - (h) Non-development software items?

Checklist 2.2

Documentation

- Has documentation for the Functional baseline been defined and allocated?
- Has documentation for the Allocated baseline been defined and allocated?
- Has documentation for the Product baseline been defined and allocated?
- Has documentation for Developmental Configuration baselines been defined and allocated?
- Have procedures for date/time stamping of all documentation been defined?
- Have procedures been established for the creation of an automated documentation library?

Checklist 2.3

Configuration items — also called computer software configuration items

- Are all computer software components (CSCs) identified?
- Are all computer software units (CSUs) identified?
- Have procedures been established for the project unique identification of all CSCs, CSUs and CSCIs?
- Have these procedures been published and made public knowledge?
- Have procedures for date/time stamping of all CSCIs, CSCs and CSUs been defined?
- Are all procedures defined in a manner which is readily auditable?
- Have these procedures been implemented?

Checklist 2.4

Revision/version identities

- Have procedures for identification of all revisions been defined?
- Have procedures for identification of all versions been defined?
- Have these procedures been published and made public knowledge?
- Have procedures for date/time stamping of all versions been defined?
- Are all procedures defined in a manner which is readily auditable?
- Have these procedures been implemented?

Checklist 2.5   Configuration of software documentation and media

General

- Have the items which will need to be distributed been identified and defined?
- Have the parties to whom these items will be distributed been identified?
- Has the purpose of the system and the function of the computers been clearly defined?
- Have procedures for document distribution been created and put in place?
- Have procedures for media distribution been created and put in place?
- Have these distribution procedures been published and made public?
- Have procedures to ensure that unauthorized distribution of documents and/or media cannot happen been created and put in place?

Document Distribution

- Have interfaces between the document distribution function and the System/Software Configuration Management function been defined for purposes of document distribution?
- Have backup procedures been defined and implemented for all documents before their distribution, including:
  - off-site storage?
  - storage in a fireproof safe?
  - periodicity?
- Have identification procedures been established for documents prior to distribution?
- Have the procedures for distribution of system documents to internal project personnel been clearly defined?
- Have access traceability and limitation procedures been created for the project and its documents?
- Have procedures been defined for distribution of documents to non-project personnel?
- Have the procedures for distribution of system documents to external project personnel (government or regulating, client, user or otherwise) been clearly defined?

Media

- Have procedures for date/time stamping of all media been defined?
- Have procedures for externally labelling all media been defined?
- Have these procedures been published and made public knowledge?

- Are all procedures defined in a manner which is readily auditable?
- Have these procedures been implemented?
- Have interfaces between the corporate Configuration Management function and the media distribution been defined for the project?
  (*Note*: Corporate Configuration Management generally limits to hardware orientation.)
- Have the interfaces between the media distribution function and the System/Software Configuration Management function been defined for purposes of media distribution?
- Have backup procedures been defined and implemented for all media before their distribution, including:
  - off-site storage?
  - storage in a fireproof safe?
  - periodicity?
- Have labelling procedures been defined for all media, and implemented rigorously by Configuration Management?
- Can all distribution of project media be traced as to sender and receiver?
- Have the procedures for distribution of system media to external (government or otherwise) project personnel been clearly defined?

3

SOFTWARE CONFIGURATION CONTROL

WHAT IS CONTROL?

A dictionary definition of control is: '. . . to restrain, regulate or constrain'. This is applicable to our discussion. Don Reifer defined configuration control in the mid-1980s as '. . . simply the control of changes to configuration documentation, hardware and software/firmware' (see Appendix 2: Reports). Perhaps it is just outdated, but this seems rather simplistic today. We have stated that Software Configuration Management is a *discipline* intended to *facilitate* the *management* of *projects*. What has traditionally troubled projects more than all other aspects is uncontrolled change. This means that in order to control software, the process of change must be controlled. Once the parts of the software system have been identified, it becomes imperative that restraints be placed upon the occurrence of the unknown. This restraint is implemented via the configuration control activity (which is, of course, the second 'part' of Configuration Management).

The IEEE formal definition of the process is as follows:

> *Configuration control*: An element of configuration management, consisting of the evaluation, coordination, approval or disapproval, and implementation of changes to configuration items after formal establishment of their configuration identification.

Now that the concept is understood, what are we going to want to do with it? While setting up the configuration management scheme for the organization of the project, the first thing will be that levels of control must be defined. Remember! *What you identified you must control*. In the previous chapter, identification authority was discussed. Now we must go beyond this. All responsibilities need to be defined. Also, levels of authority may change for different sources of change or various subsystems. (A 'subsystem' is an aggregate of software parts. This is called a 'computer program configuration item' — CPCI — or 'Computer Software Configuration Item' – CSCI — in the terminology used by the US Department of Defense.)

An important initial step is the establishment of the guidelines to be used. Schemes must be defined for: relating file identification to document identification; relating software identification to hardware identification (this is for real-time: management information systems will generally not be concerned with this issue); third-party software identification and how this is to be enforced; identification and handling of reused (or reusable) software and for support software.

Certain support elements are going to be needed if this is going to function reasonably in the complex environments being handled today. These tools can be classified into two types, procedures and software tools. Unlike software configuration identification, which does not readily lend itself to computerization, configuration control should almost always be computerized. There are a great many computerized tools on the market. The system which this book is going to use for illustrative purposes is called PVCS (Polytron Version Control System). This system, marketed by the Intersolv Corporation, is the most widely installed tool of the kind, controlling some 85–90% of the international market for this type of tool. (The Polytron Corporation was purchased by Sage Software which later changed its name to Intersolv.)

The tool functions on many different platforms (which explains somewhat its market proliferation) including DOS, with or without Microsoft Windows, OS/2 and many workstations.

As is usual when something is so widely used, the tool is supportive of the functions with which we need to concern ourselves for Software Configuration Management. Change control is never easy. However, when organized well and supported by a good tool, it can be almost painless.

Procedures, on the other hand, are an unsolved problem. Some companies use procedures (particularly common for military system development) while others use a Software Configuration Management Plan (SCMP). If procedures are to be used, there are two basic procedures which always need to be established: a 'problem reporting and change control procedure' and a 'procedure for establishment of the CCB' (Change Control Board). In addition, there are many other procedures which are optional. These include: Configuration Management reporting; configuration auditing; software development library procedures; document and media storage, handling and release and/or a procedure for non-deliverables. This list is certainly not exhaustive. In the vast majority of situations, organizations do not need to establish such procedures. They can be handled more conveniently within the framework of a Software Configuration Management Plan (SCMP). Chapters 10, 11, 12 and 13 discuss this plan in much more detail.

Finally, what is software configuration control? It is the techniques with which management orchestrates processes by which the software portion of a system achieves and maintains a visible structure (components and relationships) throughout the system life-cycle (from conception through retirement). It provides the procedures, documentation and organizational structure for control of the system implementation process. The objective is controlled, evolutionary change — growth of a system through control — via orderly management planning as opposed to revolutionary change or the unexpected or unplanned modification of a system.

Checklist 3.1   Flow of configuration control

- Are all the methods, techniques and tools to be used for controlling the flow of control for problem reports described?
- Are all the methods, techniques and tools to be used for controlling the flow of control for change reports described?
- Are all and any additional controls needed by the project identified?
- Are formal procedures for the storage, handling and delivery of all software items identified?

Software Configuration Management and, particularly, software configuration control, solves three of the most common problems facing software developers: the shared data problem; the double maintenance problem; and the simultaneous update problem. These problems are discussed in the following three subsections.

THE SHARED DATA PROBLEM

An extremely desirable and common method of organizing software development is for several programmers or projects to share modules of code, documentation, specifications, etc. This sharing of common deliverables reduces development costs. However, what happens when a bug is discovered (or created) in one of these common development objects — particularly when it is for one (only one) of the projects which use it? We call this the 'shared data problem'.

Let us say that Programmer 1 of Project Alpha discovers a need to update a function. This update is inserted into Module C, which happens to be in a 'public' library; that is, it is part of the common code. This fact may or may not be known to the programmer (Fig. 3.1).

Programmer 2 of Project Beta experiences a new system failure. That is, a new bug has either crept in or is newly discovered. The questions to be asked are: Who changed

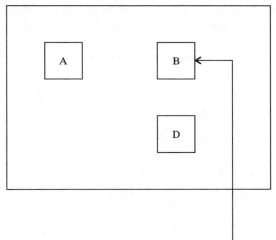

Figure 3.1   Programmer 1 modifies module B.

modules in Project Beta? What modules, exactly, have been changed? Why was there a change in the common code? Were these changes made lately? *Nobody knows!* What we certainly must be able to discover, hopefully very quickly, is that modules B and C are shared by both projects (Fig. 3.2).

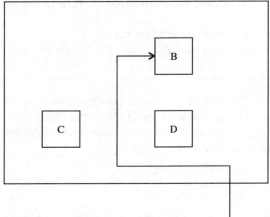

Figure 3.2   Programmer 2 has a system failure.

Experience has shown the methods which can be used to solve this problem. The problem actually has several aspects. Traceability: acquisition of information pertaining to the events which led up to the creation of the problem (who, what, when and why). Visibility: ability to discover what the actual problem is, and as quickly as possible. Finally, how can the knowledge gained be utilized to aid us in preventing this from happening again?

The trivial method of solving this problem is to have separate copies of each workfile. Quite simple. However, this means that we have lost the benefit of shared code. This solution increases overall costs. Obviously the trivial solution will be suitable for trivial systems. A better solution would be to store a single copy of the common files, but for the programmers to work in separate workspaces (Fig. 3.3). However, this introduces a new difficulty. How can we be certain that Programmer 1 will be aware that Programmer 2 must be notified that the common file has changed? This introduces the 'double maintenance problem'.

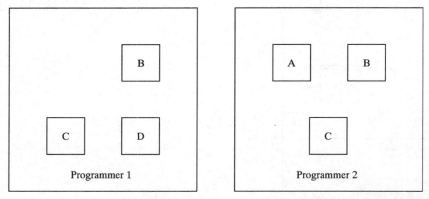

Figure 3.3   The shared data problem solved by using individual workspaces.

THE DOUBLE MAINTENANCE PROBLEM

Double maintenance refers to a need to maintain multiple copies of a file, while intending that all copies remain identical. This task can be very onerous. Not only is the overall problem trying and difficult but it is nearly impossible to ensure integrity of the systems over time. Synchronization of modules which are meant to be common rapidly becomes impractical if multiple copies are in use. That is, when a particular module is intended to be identical to another copy of the module, but they are stored separately, it simply is not practical to depend upon synchronization. A situation where a module is common to several projects, and each programmer must retain his/her 'personal' copy, creates more problems than it solves. When a problem is discovered, who is responsible for coordinating the fix in all copies? Can a 'where used' list be maintained or even created? Figure 3.4 shows this.

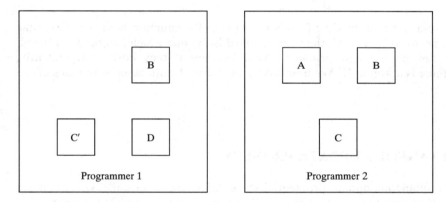

Figure 3.4   Both programmers have copies of B and C. Module C has a bug!

Now let us examine a 'typical' scenario. Programmer 1 discovers the existence of a problem (some sort of a 'bug') and fixes his copy of C. Programmer 2 still has the previous revision, with the bug. Programmer 1 forgot to tell Programmer 2 (if indeed he was aware that this was necessary) that their copy needed to be updated. Programmer 2 continues to use module C in its unrepaired state. (It may be important to note that this may not cause any 'direct' problems. Perhaps the problem discovered by Programmer 1 is not relevant to Programmer 2's use of the module.) We now have two different modules rather than copies of the same. If someone 'straightens up', these identically named modules may be copied, one onto the other. This may be quite unpleasantly surprising. The recipient of the surprise will be the one the file is copied onto. That is, it is unpredictable!

This is certainly not an uncommon situation. Fortunately, a ready solution is available (Fig. 3.5).

This solution is provided via the use of a technique called 'baselining'. Baselining refers to a system of technical organization whereby each programmer draws a copy of the needed common modules from a common base — and returns it to this base when the work task is completed.

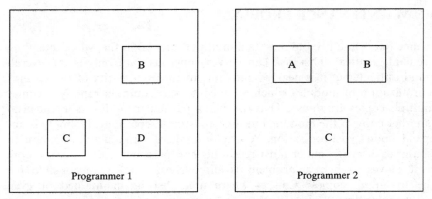

Figure 3.5 The double maintenance problem solved using baselines and archives.

When Programmer 1 fixes module C, it is returned to the common base. The next time Programmer 2 needs to look at C, the copy received is the one which has been corrected. However, we now have a new problem. What happens if they both, independently, discover that there is a bug in C? We now have a problem of simultaneous updates of the module.

THE SIMULTANEOUS UPDATE PROBLEM

What is the simultaneous update problem? Let us define the situation. Two (or more) programmers are assigned to a certain project. They share a single copy of a program file, in a common baselined archive (sometimes called a logfile). Now:

1. The first programmer discovers a bug and withdraws a copy of the module (say, 'C' again) for updating.
2. Sometime afterwards, Programmer 2 is assigned to enhance her subsystem. Part of her enhancement involves the same module.
3. Programmer 1 fixes his bug and returns the corrected module to the base.
4. Programmer 2 completes her update and returns her copy of the module to the base.

The problem now is that Programmer 1 'checks in' the updated file with the bug repaired. Programmer 2 'checks in' the same file with her updates (which, of course, have not taken into account the bug discovered by Programmer 1, as this information was not communicated or coordinated) (Fig. 3.6).

The result is that Programmer 2 has now overwritten module C, as recorded previously (Fig. 3.7). Thus the work performed by Programmer 1 upon module C has been destroyed!

Fortunately, there are clear, known and inexpensive methods to overcome and, indeed, to prevent, these problems — all at once and together. A modern, automated Software Configuration Management toolset does this in a very straightforward manner.

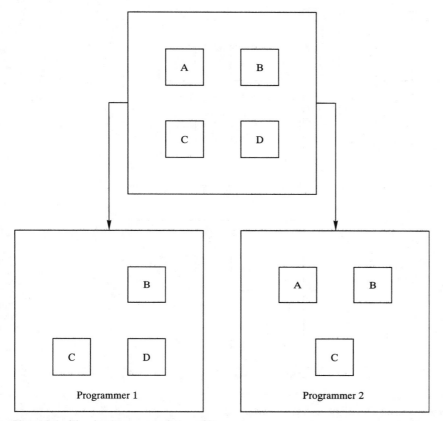

Figure 3.6   The simultaneous update problem.

BENEFITS OF AUTOMATED SOFTWARE CONFIGURATION MANAGEMENT

Actually, in all development and maintenance activities, Software Configuration Management is always performed, even for very small systems. However, sometimes it is performed manually and sometimes automatically (computerized). How should we go about deciding what is suitable for our project? Figure 3.8 helps to summarize some of these ideas.

The most important point to remember is that as soon as multiple people are on the project, or several projects use common configuration items or resources, a lack of computerized 'enforcement' makes attaining product integrity very difficult. As computerized tools are not very expensive (certainly not when compared with the alternative) there is seldom any good reason to do it any other way.

The techniques involved are: file locking; and branches and merges. These can only be implemented with the use of an automated SCM system. The point is to prevent surprises. What kinds of surprises must we demand that the automated SCM system prevent?

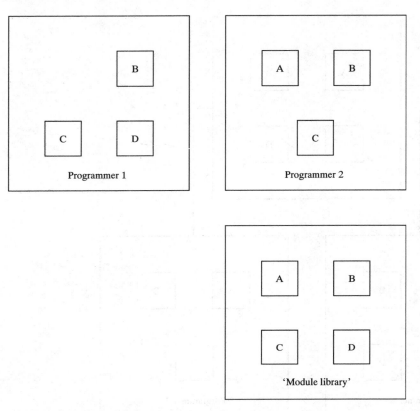

Figure 3.7 The resulting common library, with C overwritten.

Automatic	Manual
Good for:	Good for:
• large projects	• small projects
• ensuring compliance	• individual projects
• project structuring	• home use
Bad for:	Bad for:
• small, one-person projects	• heavy use
	• many loopholes
	• a large quantity of small, related things

Figure 3.8 Automated versus manual Configuration Management.

- Lack of information about changes
- Recurrence of bugs ('I fixed that one already!')
- Confusions resulting from conflicting changes
- Unauthorized changes
- Difficulties is reconstructing old versions
- Incomplete or inaccurate build attempts
- Confusions resulting from a build which used (say) the wrong version of the compiler

Let us examine in more detail what these functions are and some of their ramifications.

FILE LOCKING

What is file locking? Simply put, it is the presence of a control function which records that a 'file' has been requested by someone, and that that someone is intending to make changes to the file. Of course, this has further ramifications. If this information has been recorded then we possess a facility for coordination. Secondly, a facility to track who is making changes is also fundamental. This can also be used to prevent or control inadvertent and/or unauthorized file changes. And finally, file locking prevents simultaneous updating. Let us view an example.

Figures 3.9 and 3.10 describe some of these aspects. Figure 3.11 fills them out somewhat.

Programmer 1 checks out a copy of module C for editing. This locks the archive (sometimes called a logfile) version so that no one else may make any changes to the same copy. (Note that if this is a reasonable SCM system, previous versions may be worked on.) Changes cannot be made, but Programmer 2 may certainly view it if needed (see Fig. 3.9).

At this point, Programmer 1 checks a repaired version of module C back into the baseline (see Fig. 3.10). His own local copy is removed from the disc to prevent inadvertent discrepancies. This action removes the lock which had been in place upon the module, freeing it up for unlimited access by Programmer 2 (Fig. 3.11). Programmer 2 now checks out her own copy of C for edit, again locking the archive. Programmer 2 makes all the changes necessary and checks the module back in. Programmer 1's changes are intact, as are those of Programmer 2.

BRANCHES AND MERGES

The larger a project (or product or system) is the greater the degree of flexibility which will be needed to develop and maintain it. As has been stated above, the method for ensuring this degree of flexibility is through branches and merges. Just as file locking ensures synchronization between programmers, branches allow parallel lines of development to be performed. These parallel lines can then be prepared for later merging, if this is deemed needed (the lines can remain parallel if there is a good reason not to merge). Merges means that these simultaneous edits can be joined later. Thus, multiple, emergency bugs can be repaired and 'folded in' later. This technique, or facility, allows multiple workers on the same file. Once again, let us look at an illustration to help visualize the meaning of this (Figs 3.12–3.15).

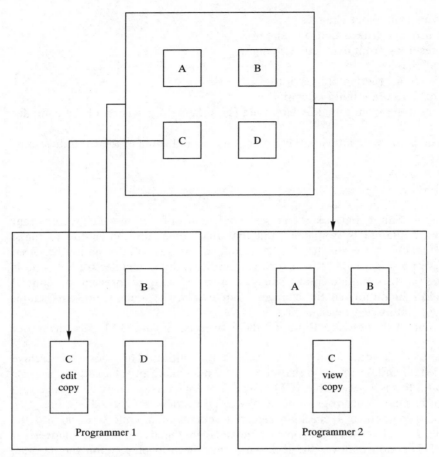

Figure 3.9 Locks.

Programmer 1 checks out a copy of module C for edit, locking the archive. Programmer 2 has need of an editable copy for an emergency repair update. She creates a branch in the archive and checks out a copy for editing (Fig. 3.12).

Both programmers make their changes and wish to check their copies back in. Programmer 1 will check his into the trunk. Programmer 2 checks her workfile into a branch revision (Fig. 3.13).

Programmer 2, with the full knowledge of what has been done, can then merge the two branch revisions to a new trunk. The merge process is semi-automatic, and flags any conflicts which may occur. After the merge, the workfile is checked into the baseline and a new revision of the archive is created. All changes made by both programmers are preserved, while the tasks were performed in parallel, saving much valuable time. (Fig. 3.14).

Branches provide both flexibility in the development process and enhanced control of this process. Of course, revision numbers, both the 'simple' kind and the 'expanded' branch revision numbers, are computed automatically by the system (Fig. 3.15).

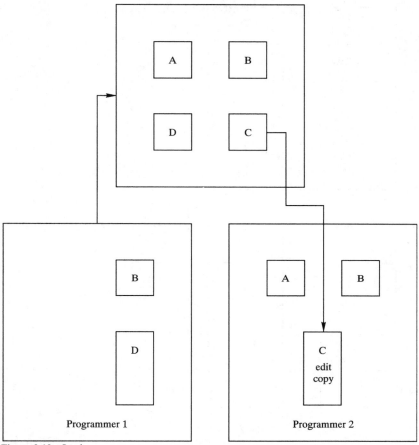

Figure 3.10   Locks.

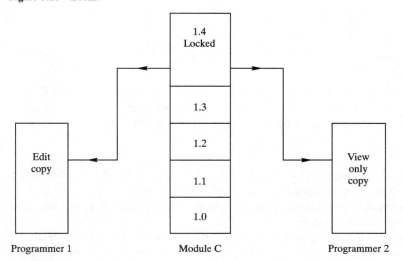

Figure 3.11   File locking.

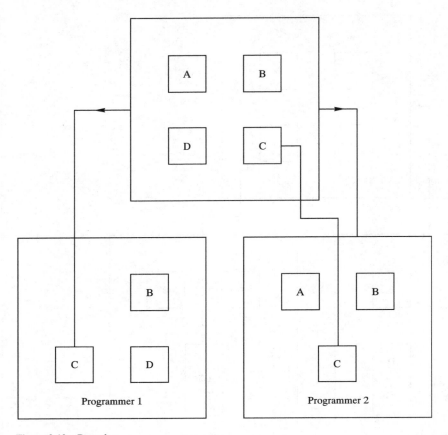

Figure 3.12 Branches.

Checklist 3.2

Configuration control

Baselines (functional and allocated), pre-PDR evaluation, pre-CDR evaluation, pre-coding and integration evaluation, pre-subsystem release evaluation, access control, change control, deviations and waivers and trouble reports control

Functional baseline

- Have the Software Development Plan, the Software Configuration Management Plan and the Software Quality Assurance Plan been placed under configuration control?
- Have the system/segment specification and the system/segment design document been placed under configuration control?
- Have the preliminary software requirements specifications for each CSCI and the preliminary interface requirements specifications for each identified interface been placed under configuration control?

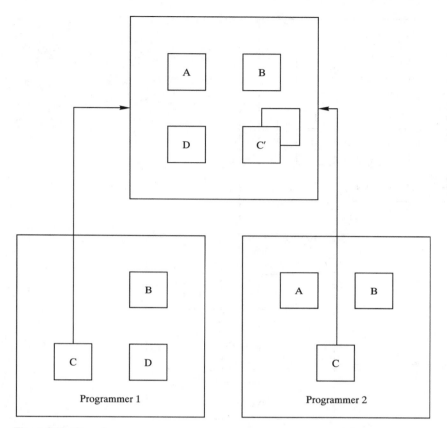

Figure 3.13   Branches.

Allocated baseline

- Have the software requirements specifications for each CSCI been placed under configuration control?
- Have the interface requirements specifications for each identified interface been placed under configuration control?

Prior to Preliminary Design Review (PDR)

- Have the software design documents for each CSCI been incorporated into the developmental configuration for control?
- Has the software test plan been placed under configuration control?
- Have the preliminary interface design documents for each identified interface been placed under configuration control?

Prior to Critical (Detailed) Design Review (CDR)

- Have the updated software design documents for each CSCI been incorporated into the development library for configuration control?

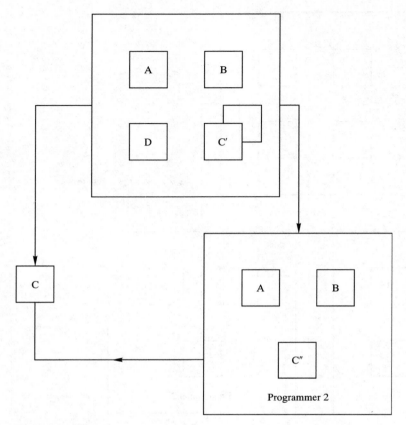

Figure 3.14   Branches.

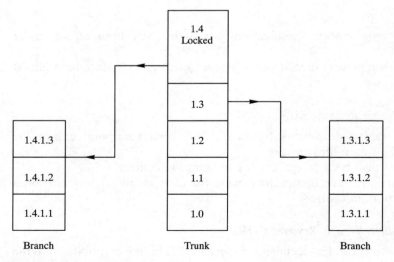

Figure 3.15   Branches.

- Have updated interface design documents been placed under configuration control?
- Have all software test description documents been placed under configuration control?

Coding, testing and integration

- Have the updated software design documents and source code listings, for each CSU which has been tested without discovered faults, been allocated to the appropriate developmental configuration?
- Has the source code for each CSU been placed under configuration control?

Subsystem (CSCI) release

- Is each CSCI version to be delivered identified via a version description document?
- Has the software product specification for each CSCI been incorporated into the product baseline?
- Has the CSCI's developmental configuration area been 'cleaned up' (i.e. superfluous information created during development must be caused to cease to exist)?
- Has the project documentation library been updated with all relevant development information?

Access control

- Have controlled methods of access to all developmental configurations and baselines been defined?
- Have all access controls been planned according to instructions of the security officer?

Change control

- Have change control procedures for all computer components (CSCIs, CSCs and CSUs) been defined?
- Have change control procedures for all documentation been defined?
- Have these change control procedures been adequately implemented?

Deviations and waivers

- Have deviation and waivers procedures for all computer components (CSCIs, CSCs and CSUs) been defined?
- Have deviations and waivers procedures for standards been defined?
- Have the deviations and waivers procedures been implemented?

Trouble report control

- Have trouble reporting procedures for all computer components (CSCIs, CSCs and CSUs) been defined and adequately implemented?
- Are all reported trouble reports traceable throughout all their processing?

SOFTWARE CONFIGURATION MANAGEMENT IN AN OBJECT-ORIENTED PROGRAMMING ENVIRONMENT

Software Configuration Management examines and handles discrete objects. This has been discussed by this book extensively whenever the concept of 'granularity' is examined. However, it behoves the developer, and the developer's management, to be aware of a few aspects which have the potential to be cross-fertile when handled correctly. Conversely, they can also be quite hindering and annoying if incorrectly used. What is mostly of significance here is that SCM is essentially object-oriented. All that remains is to use this feature when it is convenient. If this philosophical concept is not convenient, ignore it. If everything is understood, this is of no real importance.

This small subsection serves to provide some pointers concerning that important buzz-word of this decade, object-oriented. It is interesting that, in a very real sense, all of SCM is object-oriented by nature. The nature of object-oriented analysis/design and/or programming bases much of its central philosophy on internal and external reusability of defined units. Clearly, in the case of object-oriented programming, these units are units of code. In this case, these units are called 'code objects'. Many object-oriented programs are constructed using groups of code objects in different ways. These objects have been pre-planned to be reusable and will usually be called 'classes' of objects. The meaning of this — why this philosophy could have an effect on SCM — will become apparent soon.

Generally, when one envisions the primary process of SCM, one would tend to think of a system which is composed of a set of modules. Each module has been created via a series of events. Each event represents a process of a module having been revised (changed). That is, a module is a code-list and a set of revision information objects — deltas. Delta stacked upon delta, of some arbitrary length. The events may have been linear or performed in parallel: the event sequence is not of basic importance.

If this is the real picture of the process, then the SCM system must be more than simply smart enough to just pull out any arbitrary revision. The system must be able to clearly specify a particular iteration of an object and all of its associate parts which may very well come from an arbitrarily large number of files. There must be no artificial limitations on the way versions can be labelled, including 'historical' objects. Of course, an historical object is a different class of an existing object.

The SCM system must also aid object-oriented programming through branching and merging. When an object is changed to produce a new class, one should simply branch the line of development. There may be a certain price to pay in terms of the SCM system's efficiency, but this can be lived with in today's development environments. When the time comes that the module is ripe for merging, the system must allow this to happen as painlessly as possible. Also, of course, these merged objects may now be new objects, without loss of the old object, thanks to the SCM system and the accessibility that this offers.

Therefore, we see that object-oriented programming techniques are greatly enhanced through intelligent Software Configuration Management. Furthermore, flexible version labelling, together with branching and merging, allows the system to support this technique and enhance its power. One of the future directions SCM systems are going to have to take will be a more sophisticated approach to examining the internal parts of a module — perhaps control and logic information. This will reduce the maximum practical granularity from a file (as it is today) to any arbitrary level, flexibly.

In any case, we see that the object-oriented approach is a natural part of SCM. Specifically, it is philosophically a part of configuration control, hence the inclusion of it in this chapter rather than devoting a separate chapter to the subject.

All this is organized around a concept usually called 'version modelling'. There is an alternative model, one which may be preferable in many cases, this is called the 'change model'. The version model, particularly as implemented by PVCS, CCC, etc., is limited. Essentially, it knows how to handle the history of an individual piece of development, e.g. a file. There is no way to record an event which has occurred to a whole 'sub-tree'. The change model (as implemented by IntoSoft's 'All Change' – the only commercial implementation this author has discovered in 20 years of searching) allows SCM to a whole system. Any node in the tree, at any hierarchial level, may be named and can have information such as changes attached to it.

4

CHANGE PROCESSING AND CONTROL

CHANGE IS WHAT MAKES IT ALL POSSIBLE!

Certainly, the ability to make changes relatively rapidly is what makes software attractive. It is the very *raison d'être* for the existence of software. It is, however, at the same time, the most difficult aspect of software development. Even more than that, while software cannot by its nature 'wear down' it can, and does, deteriorate (in terms of its inherent quality) by incomplete or less-than-competent changes. This is a little known but very harshly felt aspect of the software phenomenon.

Over the years, experience has taught professional software developers a few lessons about the process of change and the rules that need to govern it. The control of the change process requires certain sets of documentation (usually denoted by some permutation of the name 'Change Request' documents). These requests must be recorded and processed. A set of procedures needs to be used for implementing changes to all the various types of 'products' which the project produces, and perhaps delivers. These objects include such things as code, specifications, documentation, etc. The objects may be produced in-house or in the field and they may be 'consumed' in-house or in the field. The total impact of the proposed change must be analysable. Finally, the change, as implemented, must be verifiable.

The procedures mentioned above are always discussed as a set of procedures, because *no single procedure can cover all levels of change and approval*. A common format for these procedures may be part of the Software Development Plan (such as we find here in Chapter 12) or part of a Software Configuration Management Plan (such as we find here in Chapter 13). At very least, the procedure must have provision for different types of modifications. For instance, there are usually *ad hoc* modifications which need to be made very quickly. This should certainly be the exception and not the rule, but it is not possible to expect them not to occur. No plan is realistic if it does not provide for an 'exception handling procedure', as part of the development technology.

34

Not all suggested changes are desirable. The change request must be evaluated before proceeding to implementation. To do this, the kinds of information needed to approve implementation of a change must be defined as rigorously as the project can allow.

Just as the kinds of information must be known, request routing (i.e. who needs to know, and approve, before a change ought to occur) must also be clearly defined.

Lastly, there are various kinds of things (objects) which may be changed. Clearly, something which has a greater impact upon the system must be 'change managed' more carefully than something with a lesser impact. For instance, the controls to be used for libraries will probably be more formal (i.e. rigorous) than those for a simple code module.

The change request documentation must include a minimum set of information for this critical task to be effective. This must include a clear statement of the perceived problem or 'requirement change' which has caused the change request; and why this has led to a request for a change. The documents and other configuration items which are likely to be affected by the change must be explicitly listed. If possible, the requester should try to provide a proposed solution. Finally, a process of approvals for the implementation of the change must be followed. This process will grow more rigorous as the project grows in size and complexity. Of course, as in any task of this sort, more rigorous also means more complex.

Change history, the recording of the events which have led an object from state A to state B, must be both accurate and accessible to all personnel who may have a need for such information. This change history must contain, at least, the following details for each event:

- *Who* made the change? 'Who' means owner and author identification details. These details include who created, or was responsible for the creation of, the module. Who 'owns' the module today? And, of course, who authored this particular change?
- *What* changes have been made? At very least, some sort of detailed reporting of the exact difference (or list of differences) between the present state of the object and some past state being used for comparison (some former baseline).
- *Why* were the changes made? A simple explanation is sufficient. Perhaps even a reference to a written change notification.
- *When* were the changes made? That means, date/time stamps. Each and every change of the system/object must have a date/time stamp. Also, each and every revision has its own date/time stamp. The revision creation date (the date that updating of the object has caused this revision to be created from the previous) is restored upon retrieval of the object. In addition, the archive file has its own stamp. In short, all SCM is time-critical and time-dependent.

All this leads into the documentation for the changes. The documentation should be based upon simplicity. There are three basic processes of problem or change identification: identifying the issue, the problem or change description and a trace of who approved the implementation of the change. In parallel with this, the forms used may be: a software change request form (SCR), a problem report form (PR) and a software change notice (SCN) (Fig. 4.1).

Another of the uses of the stamp is in the build process — to help make it more efficient. It is used for all file types: executable; object; source; include files; word processor files (for documentation, etc.); drawings . . . (essentially all operating systems provide this

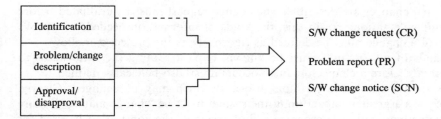

Figure 4.1 Change documentation. *Of course, these documents are for the actual processing of the change. The software configuration control system automatically ensures that all these events have been recorded on the database. It is from this database that reports are generated.*

information). This information (the date/time stamp recorded as the 'last update' of the file) is used to generate dependencies, such as: executable file from object file(s); object file from source file(s) and source file from include file(s).

The date/time stamp is used for dates comparisons:

$$\text{out-of-date} \Rightarrow \text{rebuild}$$
$$\text{up-to-date} \Rightarrow \text{no operation}$$

SPECIFICATIONS

An important and interesting aspect of Configuration Management and an aspect which is frequently overlooked — is the problems related to changes in specifications. We must remember that it is not only code which undergoes constant change. The project specifications evolve as well.

These issues are particularly important when the software of the system is developed 'remotely' — as by a contractor. Procedures must be established for preparing and responding to authentication of applicable specifications. The established procedures for submitting specifications for review — whether it is to a separate contracting agency or in-house — must allow for both verification and approval of the document, with all that this may imply. This author strongly advises that procedures be established for ensuring that all approved changes have indeed been included into all the documents affected by them. These procedures must ensure updating of all configuration status records and reports. Remember, these changes may cause new baselines to be created. A method for their approval must be approved, as well.

Case study 4.1

This author was involved in a project which spent nearly 4 years writing the specifications for a system. It was a very complex system consisting of 23 processors in various redundancy configurations. At the peak, there were 21 software and system engineers writing specifications. These specifications were revised with an alarming frequency.

At our insistence that a discipline of Configuration Management be established, management's comment was that they understood configurations of screws, not documents.

We measured and discovered that 30 per cent of the engineer's time was wasted by waiting for the word processing system to respond. This project did roll out eventually (and very successfully — even after all this their product cost less than 50 per cent of that of the competition) but a lot of heads rolled. Configuration Management was established. A SCM system was installed on a mini-computer. Two people laboured for just under two years to create the 'human engineering envelope' for the SCM. The base product chosen was CCC. They did a marvellous job. It was as a result of this experience that this author decided there must be a better tool. This search led to PVCS (though many versions ago). We did much better the next time.

What is the lesson to be learned from this case study? Is it only that SCM made the project a bit more simple to proceed with? No, clearly not! The lesson to be learned from this case study is that the implementation of SCM allowed the project to proceed at all. Twenty-three engineers writing documents is an *extremely* complex activity to manage. SCM was used to control every document from the moment that its author was willing to claim that he had finished (such, of course, was seldom actually the case). All changes to a specification document could be monitored and controlled. The quality assurance function for specifications was also made much easier.

CONTROL DOES NOT JUST 'HAPPEN'

The title of this chapter includes the word 'control.' This is not a trivial concept. We can control the process of change, but it is not easy: quite the opposite. Somehow, a quantitative handle must be arrived at. It is imperative to gain a real understanding of the quantities of changes being made. Also, it is equally important to be able to characterize and classify the changes being made in our systems: the percentage of changes made, as opposed to the changes proposed. If all proposed changes are actually implemented, this means that either the creative process has been stifled (changes are not being proposed) or too many changes are being implemented. In either case, we have lost control.

At any given point in time, project management must be capable of predicting the changes to be implemented, just as they should have a very clear idea concerning the resources being spent on the changes — as opposed both to resources used for other processes and as opposed to planned resource availability.

An interesting case in point was published in the monthly journal *Computer Design*, 1 May 1989, p. 60:

> If an FAA investigator finds written notes in the margins of an airline maintenance manual, for example, the airline is subject to a stiff fine. Mechanics don't define how aircraft should be repaired; engineers do. And they publish their decisions in change notices.

This provides a fairly good understanding of the importance of *managing change*. Change cannot be 'random'. Uncontrolled change is an invitation to crisis — an invitation to disaster. The previous example only serves to make this distressingly clear. The United States Federal Aviation Administration is quite convincingly clear about their opinions concerning uncontrolled change. In the next project that *you* manage, can you be as convincing?

These ideas also have more far-reaching consequences. They provide further proof that questions of change management and control are not specific to the developers or even to the management of the project. As a matter of fact, they are not specific to software. The change management process, if mishandled, can be just as disastrous to other kinds of systems as it can be to software. It is only the complexity of software which makes them more significant in this respect.

This process has far-reaching effects upon everyone who may be affected by the system — even those that are not actually users of it.

Just think of a banking system that can be easily changed — and then remember that those changes can be used by the unscrupulous to transfer your money to their accounts.

5

THE CHANGE CONTROL BOARD (CCB)

CHANGE COORDINATION

Generally speaking, the Change Control Board is the committee whose purpose is the control of changes. It is the critical link which will either allow changes to be managed or, if misused and badly performed, will cause (or, at least, permit) the worst kinds of confusion. It should always consist of the following 'representatives':

- A person representing the interests of the prospective system/product users/clients
- The head of 'engineering' of the project
- A representative of the management of the developing organization
- A software quality assurance representative

As needs arise, other project team members may take part in Change Control Board meetings. In any case, the Change Control Board is always empowered to summon other project team members for information-gathering purposes.

The actual size of the group must certainly be dependent upon the size and complexity of the project. For instance, on very small projects, the lead programmer should generally be sufficient for all of these. However, if at all possible, some representative of the client should be part of this 'decision loop'.

When 'designing' the Change Control Board, the principles adopted concerning committee size and functions should be based upon the old Middle Eastern saw about the committee which was formed to try to decide upon the definition of a horse — and that is how we have camels today. There are some things which must be decided by a single individual. Any simple process may be made cumbersome and obtuse by a committee. Care must be taken to avoid this kind of obfuscation — a great deal of care.

Once the basic concept of the CCB has been created ('the design of the charter') it is highly advisable that the structure selected be approved by all of the representatives listed above. Only afterwards should the people who form the committee be selected. Care should be taken that the people included have sufficient background and understanding of the project's technical and economic aspects. They must have a clear view of the ramifications of the decisions they will be making.

Additionally, as part of the formation of the group the definition of the information needs of the CCB must be codified. This will usually take the form of 'Articles of Authorization'. This must be a part of the process of definition of the committee. It must not be an afterthought, after the group has been formed. Indeed, if at all possible, this should be thought of as a basic part of the formation of the project.

IMPORTANT CCB CONSIDERATIONS

Other than the basic charter of the committee and its structure, there are also several other important points which it will behove the Board to remember and consider:

1. Make a point of defining how reused, or potentially reusable, software should be affected by changes. This is important in today's budgetary and cost structures.
2. Do security questions affect your process of change? If so, what must this effect be? (Important note: this caveat is *not* limited to the needs of military projects. Certainly, many corporations could only gain by this, the most obvious being perhaps the financial community.)
3. Source items associated with one another, with their derived object items and with sibling objects. This must be an integral part of the information base available to the committee members.
4. Decisions affecting resource allocation and scheduling should be separated from those motivated by technical and marketing issues. Then, and only then, can you justifiably present them to management!
5. Finally, remember that problems which have the potential to significantly impact operations, life-cycle costs (including maintenance) or schedules must be very carefully handled. This will usually include those problems discovered which are caused by erroneous operational requirements.

Certainly, events or problems which affect documentation only will generally be of lower priority.

Another 'ironclad' rule is that all decisions must be recorded. Table 5.1 provides a suggestion for the format of the minutes of a CCB meeting. Please note that this is a quite formal CCB, most likely for a very large project (certainly several hundred staff-years). A smaller project will have a smaller CCB and, hence, a less formal reporting structure.

As can be seen from the draft CCB meeting structure (minutes), problem reports (PR) always get separate and prior billing to change requests (CR). Basically, a problem report is a type of change request. In very formal systems (i.e. very large) problem requests may cause one or more change request(s) to be generated. However, problem requests tend to differ from 'standard' change requests in several aspects, as follows:

- Firstly, they will usually tend to have a higher priority.
- Secondly, they are usually more straightforward. That is to say, there is very little room for differences of opinion as to whether a bug needs to be fixed.

- Finally, most bug fixes tend to be easier to implement than a request for a change — which may very well need a great deal of systems analysis just to understand what needs to be done to implement it.

In any case, problem report handling must be performed with higher priority, and more carefully, than that of typical change requests, because it represents a difficulty which has already been discovered and caused someone discomfort.

Table 5.1   CCB minutes

Attendee list

1. **Purpose of meeting**
   Agenda (pre-planned and announced prior to the meeting)
     [first item: adoption of minutes of preceding meeting]
     [second item: status of decisions made at previous meeting]

2. **Reports to the CCB**
   Configuration items labelled/relabelled
   Baselining activities
   Problem reports which have been resolved (since last meeting)
   Change requests which have been closed (since last meeting)
   Disposition of problem reports
   Disposition of change requests new issues

3. **Proposals for CCB actions on new problems reported**
   New change requests
   Change request evaluation results

4. **Configuration audits**
   Supplier deficiencies
   In-house deficiencies
   Deficiency resolution plan

Distribution list

SPECIAL CIRCUMSTANCES

The Change Control Board should meet at least once per month with the full complement of permanent members. Other meetings may take place at more frequent intervals with partial membership. However, all of these meetings must be completely documented and their findings and decisions must be approved by the full Board.

During development, certain circumstances may call for needed changes at times, or with priorities, that do not allow for the delay inherent in a full committee meeting. In such a case, the software product manager may take responsibility for implementation of the change. The software product manager is responsible for justifying to the board, in writing, all actions of this nature. Under no circumstances will irreversible action be taken (such as a change of an approved item for which formal Software Configuration Management has not yet begun).

Implemented actions based upon non-approved change requests (by the Change Control Board) will be reversed to their previous state.

Non-approved change items should be returned to their originator. Such returns will be accompanied by sufficient details of reasons for the 'request denied' status that the form of an acceptable resubmittal will be clear. The originator may then resubmit the request for further processing.

Change actions approved by the Board should always be submitted for implementation through normal technical channels.

CHANGE CONTROL BOARD RESPONSIBILITIES

Each change request should be evaluated for validity by product assurance before being examined by the CCB. (This is a cost control measure. The CCB usually consists of several professionals whereas the product assurance representative will be involved by him or herself. One person's time is less expensive than several.) Further validation may be needed. If so, the CCB should resubmit the CR to product assurance for further validation with exact instructions as to the information which is lacking.

The first responsibility of the Change Control Board must include analysis of incoming change requests. The analysis must, of course, be a technical analysis of implementability and desirability of the requested change. However, in addition to these, there is an equally important evaluation which is frequently forgotten. All change requests should be evaluated for costing purposes. In cases where the change request cannot be readily cost evaluated by the Change Control Board (in session) the board should allocate the CR for evaluation by an authorized party. See Appendix 5, Attachment B: these forms provide space for the results of this evaluation.

Together with the configuration manager, the Change Control Board should validate matching of 'source items' to 'object items'. This concept of matching may have two meanings:

1. Source code to 'compiled' object code (this is the simple case); usually this will require a 'continuation trace', i.e. all relevant documents back to the ultimate (affected) requirement. In general, this concept is called 'traceability'. This is a very important concept.
2. A source document (configuration item) is compared with its derived (object) document (configuration item); for example, the document which contains the detailed design specifications for the system, which has, in turn, been derived from the system's top-level design.

Lastly, the Change Control Board must have final responsibility for *release management*. This is not, of course, the same as the kind of control that marketing may have over this function. The CCB authority over release management is technical in nature. However, as in all management areas, responsibilities must be clearly spelled out. The 'address' for problems concerning a release rests squarely upon the shoulders of the CCB!

It is crucial that the release of software and documentation, whether they are for internal use or to be released to customers, is regulated. One should even say formally regulated. This is to ensure that only the correct (hopefully, the latest) versions of all components are used.

6

SOFTWARE PROBLEM REPORT PROCESSING

PROBLEM SOLVING IS A WAY OF LIFE

Software problem report processing is, at one and the same time, both one of the most difficult activities performed by software professionals and also one of the most common. Robert Glass has stated (in discussing software maintenance) that the basic priorities of the industry are probably all wrong. The best programmers (who, rightly or wrongly, want something 'of interest') are put on development projects. Many of these projects may not really demand an extraordinary degree of professionalism or creativity, since the development of most projects is a reasonably well understood activity. On the other hand, beginning programmers are usually assigned to the maintenance of existing systems. This activity can frequently be both much more difficult professionally and much more intellectually demanding — particularly while trying to understand what some previous generation of their 'professional peers' were attempting to express, and usually without any documentation (sometimes no documentation would be preferable to the bad and misleading documentation which does exist). It is historically obvious that this assertion is quite accurate.

Despite this (apparent) reservation, it is clear that the whole software industry is driven by our ability to make changes to software (the 'soft') and that the budgets we are going to be seeing allocated during this decade will be a direct outcome of the quality of the results we produce and effectiveness of the processes used to produce them. That means, that software change is indeed, a critical activity. *Unfortunately, it is very seldom performed well.*

The activity of problem reporting is based upon two classes of problems: errors reported and anomalies discovered. All problems encountered or suggestions for new function, improvements, etc., are, in fact, aspects of either an error (in the code, in the design or in the requirements specification) or an anomaly ('. . . this is not what I had intended . . .'). A very common mistake is to think of problem reporting only in terms of coding errors (bugs) which need to be fixed. Many times, the situation is much more complex. For effective response to problem reporting, it is imperative to remember that there are many types of errors, as stated above.

Let us now look at a general procedure for handling a reported problem. The procedure (algorithm) is written in 'pseudo-code' and should be read in the customary way of following such a procedure. Indenting implies context (Table 6.1).

Table 6.1 Pseudo-code for problem response

1. The discoverer of a problem writes an SPR and the report is presented to the producer for processing.
2. The 'Customer Service Department' validates that the report is processable.
3. If the reporter is valid and the problem can be recreated THEN
    3.1 The SPR is passed to the CCB for verification and technical impact assessment.
    3.2 If the SPR is processable THEN
        3.2.1 the originator of the SPR is notified of status decisions
        3.2.2 engineering reanalyses for processing
        3.2.3 engineering reassesses (revalidates) the SPR. If engineering agrees that the SPR is valid, THEN
            3.2.3.1 The SPR's fix is scheduled for action (with the CCB) and
            3.2.3.2 budgets are allocated
            3.2.3.3 The problem is fixed (CM, test, . . .)
            END-IF
    3.2 OTHERWISE
        the originator is notified and the SPR is closed
        END-IF
        EXIT
3. OTHERWISE
    Close the SPR and notify the problem reporter that there is insufficient information for the report to be processed. Alternatively, specify to the reporter the information which appears to be needed and issue a notification that the SPR is to be closed after a specified time-out period.
    END-IF
4. Close SPR.
5. Notify originator.
EXIT

(*Note*: 'SPR' means a software problem report.)

What support software needs to exist to support this activity? ('Support software' refers to the software items and tools which are used to accomplish the tasks herein defined.) To answer this question, there is a need to describe what controls will be used to manage deliverable and non-deliverable items. Remember that hardware CM is oriented towards deliverable items only.

There is a generally accepted list of information items which should be included in the software problem report documentation, or indeed in any software change process. The following list of items is certainly quite long and yet it is probably not exhaustive. However, it does include quite a large number of data items. If your software problem report does not include all of these items, this author suggests that the list be used to check the integrity of the forms of reporting used by your organization. Not all of these items may appear (as said, this is a very extensive list). In any case, in designing a process for the processing of SPRs, one should try to take as many of these items into account (and document them) as is practical and possible — but do not go overboard.

- System or project name
- Problem number
- Problem name
- Security
- Reason for change
- Originator
- Estimation of correction effort, costs and time
- Actual correction effort, costs and time
- Deviation between estimated correction effort, costs and time and the actual investment
- Software element or document affected (expected and actual)
- Origination date
- Need date or priority
- Description of problem
- Analyst
- Date assigned
- Date completed
- Analysis time
- Recommended and alternate solution
- Implementation solution
- Impacts and configuration items affected
- Problem status
- Approvals of solution and Software Configuration Control Board decision process
- Follow-up action
- Problem corrector and all other individuals and groups with direct or indirect responsibilities
- Correction date release
- Version numbers (old and new) of all configuration items actually affected by this change

Of course, the best way to handle these questions would be to use a computerized problem reporting system. A problem reporting system must be capable of tracking all system defects (at least) and perhaps all anomalies — as reflected by all 'action items' which have been generated.

Unfortunately, high-quality systems like this seem to be quite rare. The only system/product of this kind which this author has found is called 'CMF — Configuration Management Facility'. It is produced by Expertware, Inc. from California, USA — marketed in the USA by them and in Europe by GEC Marconi Software Systems, from England. This product seems to understand problem reporting reasonably well but with very limited functionality in terms of general Software Configuration Management needs. The other functions of the system are change control and release management (see the end of the previous chapter). It seems obvious that the product is a result of a military type project. In other words, it seems to do what it does quite well. It just does not do enough.

CHANGE COSTS

The change request document (if a paper form is being used) or the CR record (if a computerized system) should be updated by the Change Control Board with the *expected* cost for the change, *before* change authorization. Or, perhaps stated more strongly, *analysis of the expected costs of implementing a change should be a precondition for authorization of the change.* Is that surprising? What this concept means is that software, like anything else, needs to have its costs *managed*. In development projects, the really bad run-away costs usually result from uncontrolled changes or uncontrolled costs of changes. Project management *and* the requester should be notified of the expected implementation costs before issuance of the authorization. In a case where the need for the change is self-evident (e.g. resulting from an obvious error/ failure in existing software, or an error discovered via a review process) this notification must not obstruct the process of change implementation and notification may be forwarded after the change has been effected. This is at the discretion of the Change Control Board chair.

Every change request contains within it two kinds of costs, which should always be examined separately. The first kind of change cost is that of the change evaluation cost. This is the number of staff-hours needed to evaluate the requested change, both in technical terms and for possible system-wide effects. The second kind of change cost is that of the change implementation cost. This is the number of staff-hours needed to fully implement the requested change. In this case, 'fully implement' means updating all documents and source-code files and full testing (including regression testing) of the updated system/subsystem.

The reader should look at the sample change request form, in Attachment B of Appendix 5. One will notice that this form contains a specific set of fields to be filled in, concerning the cost estimations. This area describes the two estimates. This is interesting. In many cases, particularly for large or strategic projects (whether military or non-military is not relevant), the cost for thorough analysis of a change may be quite high. In many cases, this cost may be significantly more than the change requester expected. Perhaps the particular change is not quite so important, after all. This is not uncommon: people just are not aware that changing software is an expensive process.

Of course, the existence of these forms and their fields is not for show. The single most important technique for cost control is follow-up. A form was used and passed on to the CR originator. A manager who does not follow this up properly is not doing the job that needs to be done. This is not optional. This is the heart and soul of good management!

In software, we are constantly engaged in managing crises. It is much better to manage to avoid their occurrence. The crisis potential is always very great. This can be reduced by proper reporting of incidents and effective follow-up. This allows management to follow problems systematically — a matter of communications. We *computniks* are supposed to know something about that. The communications must link programmers, analysts, users and management. Or in another set of terminology: the problem reporters, the potentially affected, the solvers and management (the people who sign the cheques).

PROBLEM COSTS REDUCTION

Studies have shown that fully 50 per cent of the labour invested in software is spent correcting errors. This author has checked this number on three continents, in some 10 organizations, and has found it to be quite accurate. Clearly, the reduction of these costs has the potential to quite radically change the way software is produced.

There are certain major considerations concerning the costs of problems and, of course, the reduction of these costs. These considerations are based upon the type of events that the particular problem deals with and upon the way the problems are solved. For this purpose, there are 'routine' events and 'non-routine' events. Unfortunately, most non-routine events rapidly become crises. These are the events which are very expensive.

One basic objective must be to be able to handle all events as routine — never to be in a crisis situation. One way to avoid crises is by getting problems solved. This is not quite as trivial as it may sound. If a problem is sent to the wrong person for solution, valuable time and resources are wasted. If the problem documentation is wrong, or at the wrong level of detail needed, again there will be waste. This may point to a 'problem coordinator'. We do not recommend this. The Change Control Board should be fulfilling this job — it should be the organizational body responsible for all problem coordination, at least in all 'normal' situations. Abnormal situations may exist, but they should be extremely rare.

Any long-term attempt to address problem cost reduction must be based upon a quantitative understanding of the dimensions of the situation. It is comparable to any problem with which one tries to struggle (that is, to manage).

How many problems are occurring? This is not always an easy item to count. A clear definition of a 'problem' must exist. This definition is critical for the organization if management of the change process is to be controlled. Compare the number of actual problems, the numbers of change requests and the number of changes. Which is greater? The answer to this has surprised many managers. The order of these numbers is not always as obvious as what one might expect. As a sort of trivial rule-of-thumb, if the quantities do not order themselves as you expect — start asking questions. Your initial intuition may have been too right! This certainly demands critical examination.

What is the distribution of the changes and of the problems? Distribution means when they occurred, where they occurred and certainly, to whom — to what software configuration items. Equally important for this kind of analysis, can any trends be ascertained? Are the quantities increasing, decreasing or static? Beyond this, can this information be used to aid in the striving to increase reliability and maintainability? We know that errors tend to cluster — that is, when a section of a system seems to have a rather larger number of errors, this is not a sign that we are suddenly checking better. This means that this item (or items) contains a great many more errors. As a matter of fact, when this occurs, the greater incidence of errors is probably hiding a lot more errors than are being found. This demonstrates one of the uses of this kind of analysis technique. We see here a cross-over of information from configuration management to engineering, testing and reliability. This, of course, will also inevitably lead to cost reductions.

The quantitative concept needs to inquire about resource usage. Project management needs to have a very clear understanding of the resources used, both at the present and over time. This resource usage must be measurable. These measurements need to be recorded and retained as part of the corporate productivity database. The effectiveness of this usage must also be measured, recorded and reported on.

It is certainly critical to be able to have a very clear understanding of the effectiveness of the proposed, and implemented, solutions. *There is no more stupid problem than the one which recurs.* These can usually be prevented, but only if the organization can very clearly trace that they have previously occurred. (This is usually called 'visibility'.) This is, again, a critical cost reduction issue.

Of course, another effective way to avoid a crisis situation which has been caused by a poorly implemented or poorly tested change is to back-out of the change. This, of course, implies that the Software Configuration Management system is capable of such. (Capable of accessing, effectively, previous versions of the system in a timely and resource-efficient manner.) Any SCM system which cannot do this should be disposed of — very quickly.

7

STATUS ACCOUNTING

WHAT HAPPENED? *WHEN* DID IT HAPPEN? *WHAT* WERE THE REASONS? *WHO* AUTHORIZED THE CHANGE? AND, OF COURSE, WHO PERFORMED THE CHANGE AND WHAT ITEMS WERE AFFECTED?

This is a rather long-winded title for a subsection. Basically, the main issue of Software Configuration Management is acquisition and maintenance of all information concerning a project's status and that of its parts. This status information must then be available for reporting to various levels of authority (i.e. anyone with the need to know!).

Time is always a critical part of status information. For each configuration item, regardless of whether the item is an individual item or an aggregate, a separate 'logical account' is maintained and transactions are recorded. Typically, a journal is used for recording these transactions. Hopefully, this journal is computerized and the transactions are recorded automatically. Transactions are not the only information which is recorded. In addition to the transactions, actual programming information is recorded upon the configuration item's archive. Reports are produced from the transaction log, from the archives, or from a combination of them.

Many types of reports may be planned in advance (a 'minimal' list of reports, see below). Never expect all reports to be determinable in advance. Many reports must be *ad hoc* reports. Another answer which is always to be expected from any automated Configuration Management system is a complete or partial rebuild of any older version of the system, in the exact image of what the version was. This last item may sound almost trivial but, unfortunately, there are many SCM systems which do not provide this facility.

MINIMAL LIST OF REPORTS

There are three reports which must be called the 'most basic of reports', and must *always* be available. These are:

1. Transaction log
2. Change log
3. Item 'delta' report

Some other typically common reports may frequently be:

4. Resource usage
5. 'Stock status' (status of all configuration items)
6. Changes in process
7. Deviations agreed upon

The critical points to be aware of when attempting to define reporting requirements are:

- How much formality is required by the customer?
- Who is the audience for each report?
- Are project standards subordinate to corporate standards?

Other reporting needs which should be defined as basic requirements of any SCM system include:

- Audit trail of all activity
- File revision history
- Traceability
- Quality assurance support
- Project management documentation

TYPICAL AD HOC REPORTS

Some typical *ad hoc* reports which must be expected when planning the software status accounting procedures should include the following requirements (note that in square brackets is the probable reason, need or justification for the reports):

1. Problems in release no. . . . [impact analysis, cost effectiveness, verification and validation, testing controls, quality assurance, quality metrics]
2. Number of units delivered in time period . . . [cost control, software productivity metrics, tool evaluation]
3. Changes resulting from problem no. . . . [quality assurance, complexity management, system management]
4. The logical 'tree structure' of an archive . . . [parallel lines of development]

SUGGESTED 'MINIMUM' REPORTING REQUIREMENTS

The following reports should be minimally demanded of (but not restricted to) the contractor and included for all Configuration Management activities:

- Change log
- Version delta report
- Stock status
- Changes in progress
- Transaction log

Other reports may be added on a permanent or a temporary basis at any time without updating this procedure. These reports may also include *ad hoc* reports — meaning either 'one time' or 'whimsical' reports.

CHANGE LOG

This log is implemented as an informal notebook, when lack of computing resources in a project do not allow for a better (i.e. computerized) option. For preference, in normal circumstances this log is implemented as a computerized journal. In any case, the implementation method is always dependent upon the nature of the computing resources at the contractor's disposal.

The log should contain all information relevant to, and regarding, requested changes in the system or any part (CSCI) thereof. The minimal distribution frequency of this report is monthly. Regardless of when the previous distribution of this report took place, this report will be (additionally) distributed before every formal review.

The following minimum information is recommended to be included for each entry:

- Change number:
  The change number will be assigned consecutively by the Change Control Board (CCB) and/or the configuration manager
- Change request status type:
  The status of the change request should be shown (see Table 7.1)
- Originator:
  The name, title, telephone number and designation of the person(s) or organization submitting the change request
- Software elements or documents affected:
  The specific software elements — documents or code — affected by the change, including appropriate configuration identification and version number, if applicable
- Origination date:
  The date the change is first submitted
- Description of change:
  A brief description of the submitted change
- Analyst/programmer/software engineer:
  The name, telephone number and organization of the individual responsible for implementing the change

- Expected impacts:
  The interfaces and impacts of the submitted change; including as applicable:
  (a) The impact on other systems
  (b) Configuration items
  (c) Other contractors
  (d) System resources
  (e) Training, etc.
  (f) Documentation
  (g) Hardware
- Follow-up action:
  Description of the follow-up action, the individual assigned to it and the due date

Table 7.1 Change request status types

No.	Status
1	Request opened
2	Pre-process evaluation
3	Authorized for implementation
4	In implementation
5	In pre-release testing
6	Released — originator notified of change
7	Processing suspended
8	Change request denied

DELTA REPORT

This report is generated to summarize progress of the development and to compare this progress with status presented in the previous report. Also this report displays the differences between version n of a document/module and version $n + 1$. The report should include:

- Dates:
  The dates (reporting period) of the report. For example from dd.mm.yy to dd.mm.yy
- Narrative:
  A narrative summary of work performed during the reporting period including progress of each task or unit of work as of the end of the reporting period. For example:

  Line i/module k changed on dd.mm.yy
  Change resulted from change no. [___]
  Work invested [___] staff-hours for change evaluation
  Work invested [___] staff-hours for change implementation

- Format:
  The description should be by tasks, and the breakdown of tasks and/or units of work should conform to the work breakdown structure (WBS). For example:

Additional WBS no. affected	Additional CIs affected
. . .	. . .
. . .	. . .
. . .	. . .
. . .	. . .

STOCK STATUS

This report is prepared to summarize the status of all CSCIs in the system and should include the following information:

* Inventory:
  A list of all the CSCIs in the system
  Description:
  A brief description of the status of each CSCI in the above list. This should include the version and revision designations in the development workspace and in the Configuration Management database. Also, all current and relevant documentation versions/revisions descriptors
* Location:
  The name, telephone number, and designation of the organization responsible for each CSCI

  This is a summary report: no additional information is to be added.

CHANGES IN PROGRESS

This report should summarize the status of each and all system changes which are in a defined state of 'OPEN'; and should include the following items:

* Inventory:
  A list of all the incomplete changes in the system
* Description:
  For each change, a brief description of the change should be included
* Status:
  Information related to change status
* Analyst/programmer/software engineer:
  The name, telephone number and organization of the individual responsible for the change
* Completion date:
  The date the change should be completed

TRANSACTION LOG

The transaction log is implemented as an informal notebook/journal, when lack of computing resources in a project do not allow for a better (i.e. computerized) option. Preferably — in normal circumstances — this log is implemented as a computerized journal. In any case, the implementation method is always dependent upon the nature of the computing resources at the contractor's disposal.

This log contains comments of, and concerning activities, of the project, *vis-à-vis* Configuration Management. This report should clearly show the effect and relationships resulting from each and every event (change request, change notification, etc.) which occurred during the course of the project.

The purpose of this report is project visibility.

Each entry should minimally include:

- Transaction number:
  A consecutive number for each and every entry on the log
- Date and time stamp:
  Date and time of the entry and of the event
- Originator:
  The name of the person submitting the entry in the logbook
- Software element(s) or system part(s) affected:
  The specific part of the project that this activity is related to and/or has affected
- Description of the activity:
  A brief description of the activity and conditions including relevant information
- Participants:
  The names of the persons involved in this activity
- Impact:
  The impact of this activity (if any) on other planned activities of the project
- Follow-up (if there is a necessity to follow up):
  Action(s) needed to be taken for follow-up; the name of the person assigned to follow up and the date due

Checklist 7.1 Configuration status accounting

Status

- Has the system to be employed (deployed) for the status accounting of the software configuration been identified, including contents, formats and purpose of all records and reports?
- Have a set of reports for reporting development status and progress been defined and distributed prior to this audit?
- Can the status and history of all open change requests be readily reported upon?

Traceability

- Can the full history of each component be traced for its whole development and maintenance cycle?

8

AUDIT AND REVIEWS

In the normal course of effective management, a basic function is to audit *functional capabilities* (sometimes called a 'functional audit') and *physical parts* (sometimes called a 'physical audit') of a system. The functional audit verifies system 'performance to specifications' (requirements). It is performed at the completion of a pre-designated phase in development. The physical audit verifies that all the particular items (or aggregates, or systems) that are listed as present are indeed present, and also that there are none present which are not listed. The audit is performed by a representative of management (auditors), quality assurance and/or the customer. Basically, its purpose is to ensure that the configuration documentation and the actual system are in agreement. While internal audits may be classed as essential or optional, *audits are always applied to subcontractors!* (See below.)

AUDIT CRITERIA

Every major baseline/release *must* be audited (again, certainly for items supplied by subcontractors). For in-house systems, an informal audit is usually sufficient. Formal here does not need to mean unfriendly or antagonistic: the audit function is much too important for it to be relegated to someone who is not capable of performing in a manner conducive to healthy relationships. Periodic reviews *must* be held to determine progress. Of all project management functions, change control *always* is the most important thing to audit!

AUDIT TRAIL

What does an 'audit trail' mean for us and why should it be a concern? The concept is to provide as full a project trace ('footprint') as possible. This is frequently called 'project visibility'. All Software Configuration Management activities must leave some sort of residue upon the audit trail file. This audit trail file is usually called a 'journal file'. At the very least, all modifications to any archive (sometimes called a logfile) are certainly reported. Journal files may be a universal journal (all activity) file (i.e. all activities performed by the Software Configuration Management system are reported), individual or multiple project journal files (i.e. each project has its own journal file for separate reference) or 'functional area' journal files.

Journalled, audit trail information must consist of four basic types of fields:

- The individual or group member issuing the command, i.e who issued the command
- The command which was issued
- Which archive(s) have been processed
- What actions have occurred as a result of the command

Generally, configuration auditing is best performed by an external auditor. Why? Because a very high degree of objectivity is required when auditing a critical management function. Figure 8.1 shows the audit process.

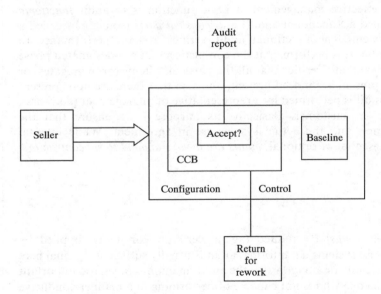

Figure 8.1 The audit process.

Checklist 8.1

- Have a series of configuration audits been formally established?
- Have the contractor's plan for support of this activity been recorded?

SUPPLIER AND SUBCONTRACTOR CONTROL

As has been stated above, items or subsystems which are subcontractor developed (or supplied) or vendor supplied must always be controlled and audited for Configuration Management. The main contractor of the project, or the customer, must be the one to determine their CM procedures.

It perhaps should even be put more strongly than that. The control of items delivered by outside agencies is *more* critical than what is actually being produced in-house! More emphasis must be placed upon the choice of the Configuration Management personnel (the question of SCM personnel is covered in Chapter 11).

The determination of subcontractor Configuration Management requirements should be governed by a consistent concept of the needs of the agency issuing the contract. These requirements must be a part of the statement of work issued to the subcontractor as part of the contract signed or order issued. The requirements must be tailored to the product being developed but as a flow-down or result of those requirements governing the whole system. All SCM requirements for the subcontractor must be a result of coordination with engineering functions, logistics and program (product) management.

As stated above, SCM requirements should certainly be adapted to the size, types and quantities of items being developed. However, it must be remembered that the overall effort spent upon the maintenance of subcontractor-supplied items, and the period of time over which this maintenance must be performed, will be no shorter than that of the system as a whole — indeed, it will be determined by that system's life-cycle. Even more so, in many instances, it will be significantly more complex, as there will certainly be 'cultural' differences between the two companies. *Under no circumstances can the demand for a computerized SCM system be relinquished vis-à-vis* the subcontractor. This is particularly true for software libraries.

> Configuration identification requirements and procedures *must* be *identical* to those of the main system.

All issues and documentation governing the configuration identification and control of *interfaces* must be very well established and frequently audited.

A clear method of change control and problem reporting must be agreed upon between the parties (the contract issuing agency and the subcontractor) and *rigidly adhered to*. This method must include progress reporting and 'open issues' lists. Also, the process of approval for subcontractor-initiated change proposals must be clearly stated and agreed upon in advance. There must be clearly defined limits upon the scope of the subcontractor's authority in everything concerning the issuing and making of changes. The issue is liability, both of the subcontractor towards the issuing agency and of the agency towards the subcontractor. Subcontractor changes represent the highest risk for uncontrolled cost escalation, schedule delays, confusion in the configuration and the receipt of unwanted and unacceptable items.

Case study 8.1

This author took part in a very large project, of which the software part was about 350 staff-years. In this project, the contractor who had received the project answered the Request For Proposal with a price quotation intentionally about 30 per cent underpriced. The intention was to make everything up (plus a large profit) from the changes to be issued. Most fortunately for the tax payer, the person in charge of the project from the side of the contract-issuing agency was a very highly competent professional. No non-approved changes were allowed to be implemented and all approved changes were paid for only after it was proven that the oversight was the issuing agency's fault.

Needless to say, the contractor lost an enormous sum of money. As I saw once as the caption to a cartoon in the *Harvard Business Review*: 'Of course, honesty is one of the better policies.' This also means that there must be a concept of liability for the implementation of unauthorized changes.

What actually are the lessons to be learned from this particular story? (Certainly a 'horror' story to the shareholders of the company.)

1. For some, evidently secret, reason which this author has never discovered, the concept of traceable liabilities is not obvious in most projects.
2. All subcontractor activities must be carefully monitored and audited, preferably by a professional team.
3. A very difficult problem is that many systems are audited either by inexperienced people or by ones who are nearing the ends of their career path with their present employer and will be in need of a position at the end of the project. This puts them (the auditors) in a position which is unfair to them.

The importance of these 'lessons' is the set of tools with which the auditors are supplied. Can they really trace everything that is happening, and has happened, with and to the system?

STANDARDS WHICH AFFECT THE AUDIT FUNCTION

Certainly, the first standard which should be mentioned in the context of software configuration auditing ought to be ISO 9000 — together with its software appendage, ISO 9000-3. Unfortunately, these documents are notoriously weak in this aspect. To be more accurate, while the subject of Configuration Management is mentioned, the auditing function is not. Additionally, the breakdown used by 9000–3 to depict the necessary functionality of SCM is certain evidence (in this author's estimation) that the authors had no real-life project experience with SCM.

Even the subsection entitled *6.1.3 Configuration management activities* fails to acknowledge the need to audit the function. While a case may be made that the auditing function is an overall management issue thoroughly covered by the standard, we see that in SCM auditing there is a great deal of emphasis placed upon the techniques. The general audit, and even the management audit, concept are totally insufficient. Every other relevant standard has clearly shown this. (See Chapter 11 for a more detailed breakdown of ISO 9000.)

The United States Department of Defense has created a set of standards for the development of software for embedded systems. The total set of US military standards for software is very large, but the majority are not within the scope of this book. The most important of these standards are:

1. DoD-Std-2167A; Military Standard; Defense System Software Development
2. DoD-Std-2168; Military Standard; Defense System Software Quality Program

On particularly large programs 'DoD-Std-480, Configuration Control — Engineering Changes, Deviations and Waivers' may also be important. However, as this last standard deals with the whole system (not particularly with software) and only with configuration control (rather than with the whole problem) we shall not consider it here.

In principle, DoD-Std-2167 defines two types of audits to be used, a 'physical configuration audit' (PCA) and a 'functional configuration audit' (FCA). The PCA verifies that all physical items are present while the FCA verifies that someone acknowledges having tested all functions against requirements.

In addition, there are three civilian (not military) standards which are very useful for understanding the audit function. These are the standards produced by the Institute of Electrical and Electronic Engineers:

1. IEEE Std-828-1983; Standard for Software Configuration Management Plans
2. IEEE Std-828-1990; Standard for Software Configuration Management Plans
3. ANSI/IEEE Std-1042-1987; Guide to Software Configuration Management

These are certainly not the only standards which exist; far from it. (See Appendix 3 for more information concerning the quantities of existing standards.) However, internationally they are, by far, the most common and the most well known standards.

9

TOOLS, TECHNIQUES AND METHODOLOGIES

PRIMARY SCM TOOL CONSIDERATIONS

There are two primary parts (and several other 'optional' ones) to any toolset needed for computerized Software Configuration Management. These basic parts are a 'revision/version manager' and a 'configuration builder' (or the 'build manager'). In addition, there are various strategies used for implementation of the tools to be found on the market today; just as there are various strategies for the 'organizational implementation' in your plant (more on this in Chapter 10).

Clearly, a critical question must be the compatibility of the various system components (i.e. the components of the Software Configuration Management system itself). This compatibility must be guaranteed by the vendor of the toolset and should be validated by the purchaser.

This is a question of the process of purchasing. This can be very simple for small, private organizations or can be quite complex in large, public organizations. It must be remembered that a 'real' Software Configuration Management system is not going to be cheap. The capital outlay is going to be quite substantial even though the actual amount (in 'absolute' terms) will be dependent upon the numbers of developers. It will be well worthwhile to make certain the purchasing process is understood, and carried out with great care. In most organizations, there will be a non-trivial amount of 'corporate politics'.

Become familiar with the purchasing procedures established by the organization. Probably, there are certain forms which need to be filled, authorizations to acquire — certainly, there is always someone who is responsible. Incomplete, inaccurate or misrouted requests will certainly cause delays. Most organizations require competitive bidding. For highly professional toolsets this may frequently be waived in lieu of a deposition by the requester that the product has been examined thoroughly and is the best for the organization. A technical specification may be requested: have this ready before it is requested. For off-the-shelf products, this should be quite straightforward. In compiling this document, provide as much information as possible. Try to facilitate the purchasing agent's task (thus hastening the process) of bid evaluation for compliance. Remember, in purchasing, as in Configuration Management, what is not documented, did not happen!

The remainder of this chapter provides explanations of the preferable functions and selection criteria to be used for SCM tools. That is, the minimally required criteria and the additional features that one should expect the toolset to implement.

THE REVISION MANAGER

The concepts of a revision manager and/or a version manager are parallel concepts and shall be treated here as one. (Refer to the definitions of these terms provided in Chapter 1, or to the Glossary — Appendix 4.) When analysing the functionality of a product for Software Configuration Management, there are two classes of functions which must be examined: functions for the support of distributed configurations and functions dealing with the toolset itself.

The most prevalent aspect of software development today is the down-sizing of the development environment to inexpensive personal computers, organized in local area networks (LAN). These networks are then somehow connected, usually via a bi-directional gateway, to a mainframe (the so-called 'client–server' relationship). This may be a simplification. Sometimes a network may be connected to other networks of various types (local area networks, wide area networks, municipal area networks, etc.). Somehow, one or more 'host' systems are communicable. What is significant here is the relationship (client–server) and the ramifications this has upon the development structure.

The SCM system positively *must* be architected for distributed developments, with support for PC-DOS, Windows and OS/2 as the most common personal computer environments and also UNIX and its heterogeneous environments. Compatibility with central computing facilities can also sometimes be significant, though this significance is constantly being reduced by the realities of working group computing.

Coordination of LAN files and LAN activities with mainframe-oriented CM tools is essential — note the differentiation between 'compatibility' and 'coordination'. This is important. Compatibility implies that the SCM system directly supports development on the mainframe, a phenomenon which is increasingly becoming rare as it is inefficient. On the other hand, coordination is commonly provided by a specialized gateway (more on this below) which allows processes to be performed in parallel.

All of this means — and heavily emphasizes — compatibility with multiple environments and multiple platforms. This is *the only way* to ensure accommodation of teams of different sizes and structures — present and future. At the same time, to truly support this sophisticated activity, there must be facilities in place to restrict activities by user or group — i.e. sophisticated access controls.

As the software world moves towards ever greater complexity and larger systems, the imperatives for reuse of software 'objects' grow constantly. This growth has encouraged many companies to define a central repository (sometimes called by various names, like 'encyclopedia' or 'depository', etc.). The most well known of these is that sponsored by the International Business Machines Corporation (IBM) called 'Repository Manager' — a part of what they call 'AD/Cycle', their life-cycle support specification. To be functional across a really broad spectra of platforms (what is called 'open') the SCM toolset should definitely conform to standards for interchange of tool information. IBM's AD/Cycle initiative is one of these. Another important initiative is the IEEE sponsored standard IEEE-Std-1175 'Trial-Use Standard Reference Model for Computing System Tool Interconnections' (this author participated in the formation of this standard). In general, the details of this field are outside the scope of this book, but it is very important to be aware of their importance when purchasing your SCM system.

The second set of requirements are those concerning the functionality of the toolset itself. Certainly, no system can be considered which does not have coverage for all development objects — i.e. source code files, documentation, graphics, object and executable files. Of course, parallel development must be supported with the control of various application versions and the ability to form development branches and to merge concurrent changes. Security and access control are needed. Sophisticated report generation and multi-dimensional 'delta reports' will aid in efforts to reduce storage requirements (no multiple copies, efficient delta storage). Multiple languages must be supported, as well as reference directories and multiple development workbenches (such as Microsoft programmer's workbench, IBM's OS/2 workstation and Micro Focus WB).

THE BUILD MANAGER

The configuration builder is a critical component of a Software Configuration Management System. Its basic function is to take the collection of modules created and to form from them a workable system. The more 'traditional' name for this tool is a make facility. However, just a make facility is no longer sufficient. That is to say, just to be able to create and recreate the system will be enough only for the simplest kinds of systems. What is really needed today is something much more sophisticated.

The configuration building tool must be compatible with the project's hierarchy. The rebuilding of software systems (including previous versions) must be easy and straightforward — but, even more than this, it must be completely repeatable! This repeatability must be reliable. A good idea for enhancing reliability is to be able to compile the makefile so that it is 'tamper-proof'. Of course, it should do this in a manner which integrates with the revision manager, utilizing file dependencies, relationships and date/time stamps. The tool, like the revision manager discussed above, *must* be compatible with multiple environments and platforms.

The specification language used by the builder (in the makefile) must be rich and expressive — allowing, for instance, mnemonic usage and macro expressions. However, it must also be compatible with industry standards to allow an ability to perform partial or full builds with a minimum of trouble. Industry standards means that it must also understand the language used by the make facility created at Bell Labs in the early 1970s for their make, and still used by the vast majority of all products on the market (most of them still use only these constructs, and they are torpid, to say the least).

TOOL IMPLEMENTATION STRATEGIES

Functionally, what does this mean about the internals of the toolset (or alternately, about the techniques used)? Minimally, it must contain a database manager, report generator and a file system for check in/check out of configuration items. Simply a 'source code control system' is obviously insufficient — this is a filing system which happens to record statistics about revisions. What we need is much more. Certainly, controlling just source is not reasonable. We must be able to store any 'member' of the project (screens, word processing files, drawings, etc.).

These basic functions must include at least all of the following:

- Tools to generate a given baseline, along with branching and merging functions
- Comparators for the programmer's use as well as 'semaphore' file locking mechanisms as protection from inadvertent concurrent update and use
- Advanced report generation, including the ability to store the report's definition
- A graphical user interface, whether this is Microsoft Windows, Motif, Presentation Manager or whatever. Preferably, it should be able to support all of them

All these and more are expressly necessary for the tool to be accepted by the programmers. Remember, if the programmers do not accept it, if it does not provide them with a rich set of aids for their use, they simply will not adopt it. It will never become a part of their development environment. There is a limit to the amount of management capital which can be spent on this.

A more advanced toolset will certainly also include:

- Change request tracking
- Facilities for the life-cycle management of each and every individual module and configuration item
- Dependency generation between mutually dependent source files and dependency definition for other, indirect, dependencies
- Object file identifications (sometimes called 'footprinting')
- Access to a local area network based library of configuration items (objects)
- Some sort of toolset which allows developers to incorporate SCM oriented functions into the application being developed (similar in concept to the use of a library of routines for database access)
- Importing of files from other, less-advanced tools
- And certainly not the last item in these days of international developments, national language support — at least for eight-bit ASCII, probably for double-byte

Remember, Software Configuration Management manages the actual items. As such, two critical questions remain which relate to strategies decided upon for disk storage of the actual configuration items, the archives. There are two combinations of two possibilities each: forward delta versus reverse delta storage and single massive databases versus individual archives. The following subsections consider some of these questions and some of the possibilities for their answers.

FORWARD DELTA

The principle of forward delta storage is that the system maintains a complete copy of the original file, as it was first presented to the configuration manager (the revision manager).

After this, the delta information is appended to the file with every PUT operation. The latest revision must always be computed before withdrawal (GET) can occur. Also, every update operation (PUTs) requires a computation of the latest revision prior to the generation of deltas for a new revision. The major problem with this strategy, of course, is that more revisions increase the retrieval time. Let us look at this, with Fig. 9.1.

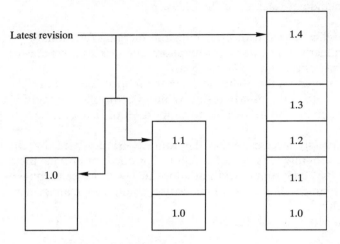

Figure 9.1 Forward deltas. Difference information is placed in the 'Tips' of the files. Change information is minimal and must be used to compute all but the first (the root) revision.

REVERSE DELTA STORAGE

Alternatively, there is the principle of reverse delta storage (Fig. 9.2). Here, the system stores the latest revision in its entirety. This means that the revision which is most often

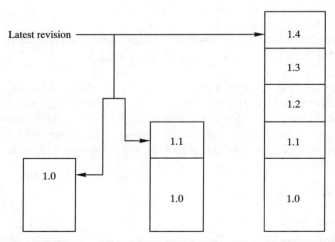

Figure 9.2 Reverse deltas. The file 'Tips' contain the most-used information. Change information is minimal but must be used to construct early revisions of a module.

needed is always available. As no computation needs to be performed, the function of updating of the archive is much faster. Finally, no computation is ever required for GETting the latest revision. Generally, this strategy has been adopted by all the latest generation tools because of its inherent efficiency.

The question of archive size is primarily determined by the ability to utilize the resources in as flexible a manner as is possible. The creation of massively large archives for storage of workfiles and deltas has proven to be counter-productive to this goal. It is both more difficult to process (longer process time) and vastly inferior to the other, residual functions, such as backups.

RECORDS RETENTION AND REPORTING

The final of the primary aspects of the SCM toolset which must be evaluated is the reporting function. Software Configuration Management is the data processing system for the process of developing software. As in any data processing system, the systems analyst must determine what information — in this case, the change history — needs to be retained and for how long.

How the information is to be stored is also of great significance. For instance, frequently need may arise for the storage and retrieval of information about the revision history. This history contains much more than just what happened. It contains *how* it happened, *why*, *when* and by *whom*. This information may (perhaps) be stored in a relational database system together with other project information (e.g. administrative, productivity, quality, etc.). This is, of course, only a possibility. Other strategies may be as legitimate, if the analysis has shown them to be justified.

The reports created from this combined data/information can make the major difference in the management of our *next* project — by learning where things went well (or otherwise) and why.

Finally, the analyst should determine whether different clients (of the application being developed) have different configurations of the product. These various configurations may be something 'obvious' (e.g. a Spanish version and a Japanese version of the same software package) or may be something much more 'serious' (e.g. completely different versions: 2.4, 3.1, 5.6). What records of these situations must be retained? For whom? For what length of time?

ADDITIONAL, SECONDARY SCM FUNCTIONS

Gateways

The term 'gateway' has become well known among local area network aficionados. It refers to the contrivance, device or facility connected on the LAN which allows the users of the network to access something which is external to it. This external 'thing' may be another computer, such as a mainframe, or another network, local or otherwise.

In our discussion, the meaning is quite similar. However, what we need to address is not just the question of access (which must of course be provided by the aforementioned gateway) but the use to which this access is put in terms of SCM. Let us see what the parts of this function need to consist of.

Firstly, we shall assume that the connection is between a LAN and a mainframe. This is not a pre-condition but is merely to simplify the discussion. The gateway must be bi-directional. That is, the SCM system on the LAN must use this to access the SCM system on the mainframe, and vice versa. The objective must be more than just mutual access. The real objective must be synchronization. This can be used to mechanize — and ensure the integrity of — the process of 'hand-off' between development and process. This permits mutual control of projects, particularly those being concurrently produced upon multiple platforms.

Interfaces to 'complementary' tools

A quality Software Configuration Management system cannot function in a 'computer vacuum'. The time of the 'screwdriver' — the individual tool running by itself without a real connection with the outside world — is simply not the reality in which modern software is developed. Today, every software tool must interface and integrate with every other tool in the developer's tool kit.

The ideal of this of course implies a fully integrated environment, perhaps similar to the AD/Cycle–Repository concept promulgated by IBM. This is not quite where the realities of technology are. It will take some years yet before this can actually happen.

It is very important that tools designed for critical management functions have the capability to 'export' information coherently and in a standard format. The most common format used today is SQL. In the future, other formulas will become more common, such as the IEEE STL standard or any of several others. The important point for this discussion is not the specific standard used, but the intercommunicability of the SCM tool chosen. This is clearly a basic principle.

A programmer's workbench

The most common of all tool types which must be integrated with the Software Configuration Management toolset is the 'programmer's workbench'. This term refers to a tool which acts as a general environment for the programmer, interfacing to all of the tools commonly used by the function of software development.

There are many tools of this type being marketed. They must certainly include, at least, a sophisticated programmable editor, with the ability to handle, in an intelligent manner, all of the various kinds of tasks usually performed by the programmer (writing code or text, compiling, debugging, testing, auditing, exploring etc.). The efficient and correct performance of these activities must allow the programmer to interface with the SCM system 'in the background'. This interface process should be unintrusive upon the thought processes and barely noticeable. Any SCM system which bogs down the programmer's job is going to be avoided.

Checklist 9.1

Software development control

Pre- and post-implementation documentation, scaffolding, programs and code, non-computerized configuration items and quality auditing

- Have the software requirements and interface specifications been baselined?
- Have all design documents been baselined after the relevant design reviews?
- Have all baselined documents (e.g. specifications, plans, etc.) been stored in the developmental configuration library?
- Have control procedures for documents in development been defined?
- Have control procedures for documentation in maintenance been defined?
- Have all development tools needed for the system been defined?
- Have all testing tools been defined, together with their relationship with the development environment?
- Have all management tools been defined, together with their relationship with the development environment?
- Have the development procedures for the installation and/or the project been defined?
- Have maintenance and control procedures for the installation and/or project been defined?
- Have control procedures for source code in development been defined?
- Have control procedures for source code in maintenance been defined?
- Have control procedures for project media been defined?
- Have off-line storage procedures been defined for backup libraries?
- Have recovery procedures been defined for libraries which have become 'damaged'?
- Have all test descriptions and procedures been baselined?
- Have all baselined test materials — descriptions, procedures and test cases — been placed under configuration control?
- Have all test results (test reports and summaries) been placed under configuration control?
- Have facilities been provided by the development environment for the non-computerized aspects of the system?
- Have all interfaces between the development environment and the non-computerized system components been clearly defined and published?
- Can development environment integrity be verified by an independent auditor?
- Has documentation of the development environment been audited?

A DEVELOPER'S TOOLKIT

An interesting bit of functionality which can be introduced today is an interface between the Software Configuration Management toolset and the programmer. This would probably take the form of a library of functions which can be dynamically linked, by the programmer, into the application being developed. This kind of interface allows the application designer to integrate version management functions within the context of the product being produced; for example, a word processing system which allows the user to define, as a parameter, the number of 'generations' to store for each document, without cluttering up the directories with unwanted files having silly names (permutations of the origin file name).

All generations of the file can be stored directly, within one physical file and under one known name. Any needed revision of the document could then be retrieved without expending undue effort. All sorts of information concerning the document is readily accessible. And finally, when prior revisions are known to be no longer of potential usefulness, they can be purged from the file, again with no significant burden being placed upon the user of the system.

This is, of course, not true only for word processing. This functionality is useful for computer-aided design (CAD) systems computer-aided software engineering (CASE) systems, software tools, program editors, computer-based training and many others.

Certainly, then, the available functions cannot be limited to only text files. Even most word processing files are not simply text: they are full of all sorts of other kinds of additional data. This library of routines must have the capability to process either text or binary files. These binary files may very well consist of images or graphics or almost anything else.

Checklist 9.2

- Have the system's boundaries, as regards the libraries to be created and managed for the development and maintenance periods, been clearly defined?
- Have these definitions been made a part of the system's specifications?
- Have unique names been defined for each separate library which is to be used and/or created?
- Has a procedure been established, published and made public, which defines naming conventions for each module within a library?
- Has the purpose of the system and the function of the computers been clearly defined?
- Have the purpose(s) of each library been clearly defined?
- Has a distinct role been defined for each library (a reason for their separation)?
- Is the software development library structured in an auditable manner?
- Do development procedures define interfaces with the software development library (e.g. the library's users)?

NON-DELIVERABLE ITEMS

One final word about this framework known as the 'techniques' of Software Configuration Management. There are frequently items created by projects which, while they are an integral part of the project, are not intended to be delivered (e.g. perhaps the structures and tools to be used for testing the system).

This is particularly true for complex embedded systems or information systems which are very large. There are many aspects of these (non-deliverable) parts which may be in need of the attention of the function of Configuration Management – of the project itself or of the contracting agency. Remember that these are configuration items, albeit of a special kind and of clearly lesser importance.

All non-deliverable items which are to be developed or purchased as part of the project must be identified and clearly labelled. Of course, they must have unique names assigned to them, just like any other configuration item. Make certain that the purposes of these items and their functions are clearly defined. Of high importance, make certain that any subcontractor's plans include coverage of all identified non-deliverable items.

Procedures must be defined for these items, even in the event of later discovery (definition) of a non-deliverable item. These procedures must be harmonized with managerial plans of all types (e.g. Software Development Plan; Software Quality Assurance Plan; Software Configuration Management Plan; Software Test Plan).

Documentation must be included. This should hopefully include requirements, operations and basic design of the item. Also, of course, testing procedures for all software, hardware and firmware items must be described, together with any procedures for quality assurance of the non-deliverable software, hardware and firmware — all this must be in accordance with recognized standards.

Figure 9.3 summarizes the classifications of Software Configuration Management.

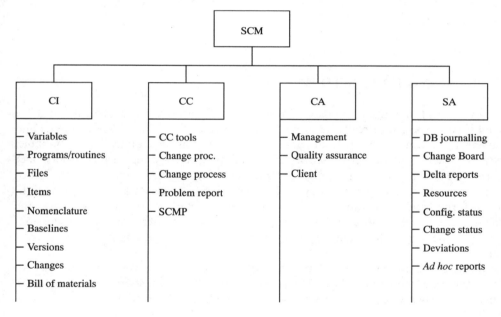

CI = Configuration identification
CC = Configuration control
CA = Configuration auditing
SA = Status accounting

Figure 9.3 Software configuration management taxonomy.

10

SOFTWARE CONFIGURATION MANAGEMENT PLANS

THE PLANNING IMPERATIVE

Like any critical management task, Software Configuration Management must be planned if you expect it to really happen. The objective of the SCM Plan is to create and document a system which will describe and specify, as accurately as is possible, everything which is to be performed by the developing agency (the primary developer and, if they exist, any secondary or subcontractors) which concerns the configuration of the system/product. This system may include additional documents to the plan itself, such as forms and procedures. (Be careful not to confuse the two systems: the application being developed by the organization is not part of this discussion. Remember, the application developed by the process under discussion is the SCM system.)

Certainly, the SCM system *must* specify a set of software tools which will be used to perform the SCM functions. While SCM can still be performed manually for small systems, the expense of a software toolset is such that it should *never* be cost-prohibitive.

Some clue as to the importance of this function may be inferred from the relative size of this chapter as compared to the book as a whole. In itself, this is the longest chapter. In addition, this chapter is followed by two related chapters, not short in themselves, providing examples which may be followed. They are sample plans which the reader may use directly or follow for producing a tailored plan for a specific project.

The objective is to briefly outline the ideas behind the process of planning the Configuration Management function, then delve deeply into details of what a plan should include, via Chapters 12 and 13. These chapters are attached to provide the necessary details for military projects and for civilian projects. Refer to whichever sample plan that satisfies your needs in either Chapter 12 or 13.

SOFTWARE CONFIGURATION MANAGEMENT PERSONNEL

Unfortunately, the majority of software engineers do not learn anything about Software Configuration Management in their university, or other basic, training. A general rule about Software Configuration Management is that an experienced systems analyst is needed to initially implement the system. However, once the SCM system has been implemented, it should be manageable by an average industrial engineering technician or someone with a background in management planning or production control.

What sort of people should we look for to implement the system? Ideally, the person we look for should be someone with a background in software quality assurance. In addition, a very good background in software development is absolutely essential. That is, an expert in the software development processes being used by the organization, hopefully, but not necessarily, including the actual applications being implemented.

Whoever is chosen, they should certainly be sent on some sort of short course (there are many such on the market) for initial training. Training must include more than just the tools with which the system is to be implemented. It must include a method for implementation, much as this guidebook does.

SYSTEM DESIGN

The system must manage a change, from discovery of the need (or problem) through to verification that it has been implemented properly. In order to *manage* change, the organization must analyse the potential impacts of the change upon program functions. Other configuration items may be impacted in many ways. Perhaps the most trivial example might be a need to change a requirement which then affects the design, a piece of code and the test cases. In many cases, the effect can be much more complex. A change in a data structure may affect all functions in a system, as well as other, interfacing, systems. All this must be analysed prior to the decision to implement. A systems engineering approach must be taken.

Total impact analysis is usually beyond the scope of a single person. This is part of the basic reason behind the formation of Change Control Boards.

Changes may also be handled differently as the project progresses. A requirement change made during the design phases certainly has a much lower cost than making the same change during the testing phase. See the following case study.

Case study 10.1

This author was involved in a large project, consisting of about 250 staff-years in software. The project 'subject' was the command and control subsystem for a national telephone system. One of the critical functions of this system was that it must be secure. The project was of a military orientation. (For obvious reasons, the client and the country will go unnamed here.)

The author's main involvement was during the phase of the project which was called 'Testing and Checkout'.

The project was receiving about 30 change requests (CRs) per week. Most of these CRs directly affected the system requirements. Management did not agree to implement Software Configuration Management, either automated or manual. As a matter of fact, they did not agree even to register the CRs as a good management practice of event recording. This author informed management that, with all due respect, without good Configuration Management, the system was doomed to dismal failure. They decided to go ahead, without SCM. This author resigned his position.

Most unfortunately, circumstances proved this author to be correct. The system eventually implemented 60 per cent of the defined system requirements, with nearly a 200 per cent budget overflow. It is not fun to be right with those kinds of results. There is no satisfaction from that.

ACTIONS TO BE TAKEN FOR SCM PLANNING

A functional block diagram should be created for the functions of Software Configuration Management. This block diagram *must* include the following functions:

- Configuration identification
- Configuration control
- Change management
- Problem reporting
- Status accounting
- Internal and external auditing

Additionally, one may also include:

- Information gathering (records retention)
- Analysis
- Processing disposition
- Implementation
- Approvals
- Verification and validation

Every organizational function must be shown. This block diagram must clearly depict all relationships of reciprocity between the functions and between these functions and the various organizational parts.

Determine in advance who the members of the CCB are to be. Obviously, this is in addition to the data requirements, terms of reference and authorizations. Keeping in mind that the committee must be kept small to function effectively, define permanent and temporary members. Define also who the basic members are, without whom the CCB cannot function. Some members may be temporaries, as the need arises. On large, real-time systems, there may be a particular need for interface control. This may require either additional members or a subcommittee.

THE SCM PLAN

As to the plan itself, and its format, this author recommends usage of the IEEE Std-828-1990: *IEEE Standard for Software Configuration Management Plans*, September 1990 (approved by ANSI, 15 February 1991).

The standard recommends a Software Configuration Management Plan to be organized in six sections, according to the type of information to be presented. Table 10.1 provides an overview of this information content and document outline.

Table 10.1 SCM plan information classification

Information class	Standard	Plan	Description
Introduction	2.1	1	Purpose, scope, terms and references
SCM management	2.2	2	Responsibilities and authorities
SCM activities	2.3	3	Activities, as applied to the project
SCM schedules	2.4	4	Coordination of SCM with project activities
SCM resources	2.5	5	Tools and physical and human resources for the execution of the plan
SCMP maintenance	2.6	6	How plan will be kept current

In many cases, this standard will be a very suitable methodology for creating the needed plan. This author, however, *very strongly recommends* that you study closely the document called IEEE Std-1042-1987: *IEEE Guide to Software Configuration Management*, 1987 (ANSI approved).

The document provides several appendices with detailed outlines for various Software Configuration Management Plans (e.g. real-time, critical projects, maintenance projects, etc.). These various examples provide a high degree of customization in very short time. In Section 3 of the document is provided one of these examples (for critical projects) expanded to include a partial information content.

AUDITING THE SCM PLAN

The SCM Plan is, of course, a document. This document serves as a tool for intelligent management of the Software Configuration Management function. Like any other management document (and, indeed, management function) this must be audited. An evaluation of the Software Configuration Management Plan may be for a whole installation or for a specific project.

It is very important to remember that this sort of evaluation may be performed for any of many reasons. Two of the most common purposes are usually either (1) that of auditing that the proper procedures are being carried out at a subcontractor's installation; or (2) when beginning the processes at an installation which has not previously had experience with this discipline. The major problem to be addressed in both of these cases is a swift and accurate collection of as much data as possible which reflects how the process is being performed. In most installations, there is a process in place to perform the task at hand.

The process may not be particularly sophisticated, and perhaps not be computerized — it does not always need to be so. Manual systems can frequently work quite adequately.

The following checklist will facilitate this evaluation procedure. The proper use of this checklist will smooth the processes involved tremendously. Examine each section of the Software Configuration Management Plan to be audited. This checklist assumes that the auditor is a professional who is familiar with aspects of the subjects as covered by this book. Before starting, examine all the questions to be asked. Do not attempt to 'second guess' the questions. After the checklist has been used, you may attempt to add questions to 'tailor' it to your environment, but do so with care. The process is as follows:

1. For each question, decide whether the question is relevant to the system, the organization, the development environment.
2. If it is relevant, decide whether the information provided by the paragraph being examined fulfils the expectations of the question.
3. Answer 'Yes', 'No' or 'Not applicable' to the question, as needed. Whether the question is relevant or not, be liberal with comments. This will allow the Plan's author to correct the document.
4. Finally, report your audit results.

Checklist 10.1

Scope of the Plan

Identification, purpose, introduction and referenced documents

- Does the document contain a cover sheet which clearly identifies it and a standard title page in the indicated format and a table of contents?
- Has the purpose of the plan and an introductory section been presented which will ensure that the reader of the document really needs to invest his or her time?
- Are all referenced documents listed by name and number?

Resources and organization

Organizational structure, personnel and resources

- Does this plan describe the organizational responsibilities of Software Configuration Management?
- Does it include the authority and responsibilities of each organization and its relationship to other organizational entities?
- Does it describe the number and skill levels of personnel that perform SCM?
- Does it identify and describe the specific resources necessary for performing SCM?

Configuration Management Activities

Configuration identification and related documentation, configuration control, reporting, review procedures, storage, handling and release of project media, configuration status accounting, configuration audits, preparation for configuration authentication

- Does this plan describe the process by which problems and changes are submitted, reviewed, and subsequently approved or disapproved?
- Does this plan identify and describe formats used to document software problems and changes detected during software development?
- Does this plan describe the methods to formally control the storage, handling and release of software documentation (including master copies) during the development process?
- Does this plan define the configuration status accounting system?
- Does this plan describe procedures for conducting configuration audits?
- Does this plan describe the contractor's procedures to prepare for and respond to authentication of the applicable specifications?
- Does this plan identify major milestones for the life-cycle phase(s) of the contractual effort?

11

AN INTRODUCTION TO THE SAMPLE SCM PLANS

THE *PLAN* AS A MANAGEMENT MILESTONE

Configuration management is exactly like the management of anything else — it is best performed in an organized manner. The best way for a process to be organized is to organize it! Hopefully, this also means that it cannot be kept secret from the people in the organization. As the previous chapter discussed, this should be done by publishing a document which defines what the process is to be and how this process should 'look and feel'.

Chapters 12 and 13 of this book contain sample Software Configuration Management Plans. Each of these chapters presents the plan according to a specific format for a plan of this sort. The formats used are *based* upon standards. The word 'based' is emphasized because the standards used are, indeed, the basis upon which they are written, but this must not be taken to mean that everything else is ignored! When writing a critical project document, a standard is extremely useful and can save a great deal of time and money. However, once the writer of such a document has gained some experience, this author strongly recommends that critical judgement be used to determine real-life applicability for some of the lower-level information demands. Also, in many cases, other additional information is needed which a specific standard may not yet demand.

The particular standards chosen are clearly the most widely used standards of the kind. This is true in America, in Europe and world-wide. As a matter of fact, although there are a large number of standards that discuss Software Configuration Management (world-wide, there are some 20 standards) there are not a large number of standards which are worth choosing from. This may be for any number of reasons, but the most common is that most such standards simply have not been designed internationally or for very wide applicability. (More on this below.)

To be more specific (as stated) many organizations, both international and national, have standards for Software Configuration Management or standards for software quality (assurance, evaluation or whatever they choose to call themselves) which contain sections on SCM. They are both beyond the scope of this book and not suitable for general usage. To provide an idea of the quantities of Software Configuration Management standards known, this author tried to find all standards which might be relevant, as reference. A total of 20 standards which discuss, in some reasonably comprehensive way, Software Configuration Management have been discovered (Table 11.1). This book does not pretend to cover all of them, nor would there be any reason for such coverage, once their unsuitability and inapplicability has been determined.

Table 11.1 Quantities of Software Configuration Management standards

International organizations	2
Professional organizations	2
Military organizations	4
Other professional societies	12

In principle, there are two possible ways of organizing a management plan for Software Configuration Management: as a separate document or as part of another, management, document. The choice is, or should be, essentially one of taste. However, many times there may be circumstances, such as a client with specific demands, which force a certain usage. There really is nothing wrong with this, as there is no clear 'break-even point' when one should be preferable over the other. However, there *are* certain criteria which may be used to direct ourselves to a more appropriate choice. We discuss some of these criteria below.

A STANDARD DEVOID OF A SCMP

Certainly, the first standard which should be mentioned in the context of SCM plans is ISO 9000, together with its software 'appendage', ISO 9000-3. (Note that in different countries these documents have various names and usages. In the United States they are called the Q90 series. In the European Community they are the 29 000 series.) Unfortunately, these standard documents are notoriously weak in Software Configuration Management. While the subject *is* mentioned by ISO 9000-3 (this is paragraph 6.1 of the standard), the 'form' and content used to depict the necessary functionality of SCM is so poorly analysed that it appears certain (in this author's view) that the standard's authors had no real-life project experience with SCM. Certainly, that statement deserves, even demands, some explanation.

ISO directs the standard user (the user of the ISO standard is called the 'supplier') that such a one '. . . should develop and implement a configuration management plan . . .' (paragraph 6.1.2). So far, this is fine. The mere fact that the standard does not direct us to a format simply makes the job that much more difficult and random. This, in itself, is not enough to direct our previous comment.

What is really wrong with the format of the standard is:

1. The list of items that the plan is to cover
2. Documents are *specifically excluded* from SCM

Let us examine each of these problems in greater detail.

The list of items that the plan should cover: ISO directs the supplier to discuss the organizations involved in SCM, the SCM activities, then tools and techniques to be used and the stage at which items are to be included under the SCM umbrella. We have seen the inadequacy of this in the previous chapters. The most glaring absences are that no mention at all is made of either status accounting or SCM auditing! This is no light matter. As we have seen, a well-designed SCM system will provide the corporation with a very important *strategic resource* and, of course, advantage. The absence of a well defined SCM auditing function — not a cursory management audit mixed in with many other audit items — almost ensures that this resource will not come to fruition.

The lack of a well designed reporting facility is even more significant. It has been stated that the analyst designing the SCM system must be highly skilled and must use these skills to ensure the design of a management information system for the process of software development. Proper reporting facilities are an imperative element of the design of any MIS, without which the system will be conceptually incomplete. This cannot and must not be left to chance. It must be an integral part of the demands for the system. With the absence of this demand, they have trivialized the SCM system and devoided it of the practical benefits which it must supply.

Differentiation between control of documents and SCM: The development of software is a learning experience — from the more abstract to the more detailed. The software is created via the development of increasingly detailed documents, their critical examination, evaluation and subsequent enhancement. These documents (the code is simply the most detailed document of them all) also form the documentation of the development process. Unfortunately, ISO 9000 still thinks like hardware manufacturers where the ultimate result of the development cycle is the 'testable' product rolling off the line. In software there are many ultimate results (e.g. a library developed for one project is used for other projects). The lack of a clearly defined demand for configuration control and management of all of a project's documents is almost a formula for disaster for any significant software project.

Additionally, many very significant professionals today emphasize the process aspect above that of the product, in particular the Software Engineering Institute's 'Capability Maturity Model for Software' (see version 1.1, CMU/SEI-93-TR-24, February 1993). No process may have its inherent quality evaluated and improved without very strict adherence to control of the documentation of the process. The SEI has defined Software Configuration Management to be as critical as quality assurance or project planning.

> The purpose of Software Configuration management is to establish and maintain the integrity of the products of the software project throughout the project's life cycle.

This includes *all* work products, i.e. documents. This author completely agrees with the criticality that this conception implies. As stated above, the standard(s) references other non-phase items in addition to Configuration Management. The other items discussed are:

6.2   *Document control* — this anomaly is discussed above.

6.3   *Quality records* — they do not really have a great deal to say, and this is certainly a great pity. All they say is that the records should exist and be accessible.

6.4   *Measurement* — with metrics they tried to be a touch more realistic. Unfortunately, a real definition of high-quality software metrics still takes a great deal of courage. The standard does not quite cut it.

6.5   *Rules, practices and conventions* — they say they should exist. Insufficient!

6.6 *Tools and techniques* — they say they should exist.

6.7 *Purchasing* — phrased as an obvious hold-over from the base standard for hardware (ISO 9001). Almost usable.

6.8 *Included software product* — phrased as an obvious hold-over from the base standard for hardware (ISO 9001). Almost usable.

6.9 *Training* — quite reasonably well done.

There are also several non-phase oriented items which should have been included and are not, the most prominent of them being risk management and technology improvement planning.

A point of clarification: ISO 9000-3 is not really a standard, though it has been referred to by that title here. The document is called 'Guidelines for the application of ISO 9001 to the development, supply and maintenance of software'. The issue date is 1 June 1991. This is called the first edition.

For these reasons, this author does not believe that the SCM coverage provided by ISO 9000-3 is truly relevant to software development in general or certainly to large projects in particular. This is most unfortunate. Do not, however, misunderstand. This author is not advocating not using ISO 9000-3. This would be counter-productive. What the user of ISO 9000-3 must do is to adopt a reasonable Software Configuration Management standard or acceptable guideline or agreed-upon procedure and adhere to it. Within the ISO 9001 documentation (which is what is checked by the auditing team for the certification process) one must define what this linkage is and prove adherence to it. This is adequate for ISO 9001 usage and correct, in terms of SCM.

Finally, to view some sample text that may prove helpful for the users of this very important standard, please refer to the Appendix of Chapter 13 — the end of the 'Corporate-Wide' Sample SCM Plan.

THE SCMP FORMAT AS PART OF ANOTHER PROJECT DOCUMENT

The first of these chapters containing a SCMP sample (Chapter 12) is based upon a format where the Software Configuration Management Plan is constructed as a part of the Software Development Plan. This is a common practice, particularly in very large projects. For instance, this is quite commonly used by military projects, though there is certainly no reason why others would not find it equally relevant. Indeed, in many cases, even for projects which are not very large, the practice is clearly preferable.

The plan which appears here is based upon a format which is a part of a particularly well known standard. The document (standard) chosen for this plan is part of the standard produced by the United States Department of Defense for embedded systems. This is known as 'DOD-STD-2167A; Military Standard; Defense System Software Development (released in 1988). This standard is widely used by all NATO countries. Our experience has shown this standard to be used in many countries and many projects (both within and outside the USA) — certainly in all countries which tend to purchase their weapons systems from the United States. This author has personally used this standard in Great Britain, The Netherlands, Singapore, Israel, Spain and South Africa. It is also noteworthy that the use of this standard is not confined to weapons systems.

Case study 11.1

In one project that this author has been involved in, the DoD-Std-2167A standard was used to aid the creation and documentation of a civilian system for a Spanish company. The reason for adoption of this standard was that the project dealt with a trainer system for a civilian aircraft — a pilot trainer. This is a highly man–machine interface intensive system. Unfortunately, 2167 is a bit weak in the area of MMI documentation (what this system was all about); this was one of the reasons why this choice was, perhaps, not quite optimal. (Not optimal does not necessarily mean that it was a bad choice.)

(Note that, despite what is commonly thought, this is a US DoD standard used on a purely European project. This is much more common than most people think.)

Regardless of the choice, or its relative 'goodness', this is a useful example of over-use of this standard. The demands which the standard placed upon the project were unnecessarily onerous. This use expanded the contract costs by a significant proportion. The planned size of the subproject (instructor station of the trainer) was just under four staff-years. The actual size was nearly seven staff-years. Most of the overshoot resulted from initial subcontractor organization (this was the company's first project). The portion devoted to 'massaging' the standard was significant, though it is important to note that both the subcontractor and the contractor were in agreement that most of this documentation was quite necessary.

Therefore, this example should not be mistaken for criticism of the standard. The standard certainly could have (and should have) been made applicable to the project via a tailoring process. *Any* standard used must be thoroughly understood by those who are to be responsible for its use. One might even say that the knowledge must be available to use it 'expertly'. This is almost never a trivial requirement, particularly for this standard.

This particular standard supersedes a previous version (by the same name) which was numbered 'DoD-Std 2167' (non 'A' — this was released in 1985). In terms of our subject matter, the important difference is their attitude towards the subject of Software Configuration Management. In the previous standard, the Software Configuration Management Plan was a separate document. This document's format was governed by the data item description called: 'Software Configuration Management Plan; DI-MCCR-80009'.

In the present version, both the Software Development Plan format, and Configuration Management, are determined by the data item description called: 'Software Development Plan; DI-MCCR-80030A.' It should be emphasized that this format is a significant improvement over the previous one and has been found to be very effective.

This author advises examination of its adaptability for many projects. It happens to be a very good format for both the development plan and, within it, the Configuration Management Plan.

There are only two caveats concerning the use of this format. One is that it is intended for use by a specific project — as opposed to a plan for an organization. If a plan is needed for the organization as a whole, then this format is not advisable. One would be advised to use the second (Chapter 13).

The other caveat is that one is in danger of overdoing things somewhat. In this connection, one must be wary of two dangers:

1. *Over commitment* — one must be very careful to avoid committing to the performance of actions which the organization cannot really live with. Or, in other words, saying more than one should because the format seems to suggest it should be said. The standard can, and should, be tailored for the use which is being made of it. Tailoring must include content.
2. *Small projects should have small plans!* Beyond the questions of tailoring discussed above, one must also take care that one does not create a monster. The size of the plan, and the effort in creating it, should reflect the size of the project creating it.

Incidentally, all of these documents (the standards and their data item descriptions) are public domain documents and not subject to any known legal or ethical restrictions concerning their use or distribution.

There is another common practice which is similar to that of including the configuration management as part of the Software Development Plan. This practice was best represented by the 1984 version of the ANSI/IEEE standard: 'ANSI/IEEE Std-730-1984; IEEE Standard for Software Quality Assurance Plans'. In this standard (which has since been replaced by a later version — IEEE Std-730-1989) an option was provided for including the SCMP as part of the Software Quality Assurance Plan. This can be cumbersome and is probably less usable than placing it within the Software Development Plan.

STANDALONE SCMP FORMATS

The second of these chapters containing a sample Software Configuration Management Plan (Chapter 13) is based upon a format where the Software Configuration Management Plan is a separate document. This format is based upon a standard created and authorized by the IEEE Software Engineering Standards Subcommittee. This subcommittee is a part of the Standards Committee and their standards production activities. The actual work on the document — both its creation and update — is performed by a working group. This working group operates as an 'authorized project' under the standards subcommittee mentioned above. (Sorry if that sounds a bit complex, but that is the hierarchy used.)

This standard has been published in two versions. The first and initial version was published in 1983 as: 'IEEE Std-828-1983; Standard for Software Configuration Management Plans'. The second version is called: 'IEEE Std-828-1990; Standard for Software Configuration Management Plans'. The differences between the versions have been described above.

In addition, the IEEE has also published a 'Guide' to aid the user of the standard. This guide is a very good, very useful document. Its official name is: 'ANSI/IEEE Std-1042-1987; Guide to Software Configuration Management'. This document is highly recommended. This author has been a part of both of these working groups since they were first formed, and remains a member to the present.

The earlier version of the standard, and also the guide, contained a specific format for the plan. This format has been used as the basis for this sample Software CM Plan (Chapter 13). The guide provides the user with more than just a simple set of guidelines for the performance of the activity. Many aspects of the activities are discussed, such as the various levels of control which one may choose.

The user is also provided with four variants depending upon the 'type' of Software Configuration Management which needs to be performed. The types defined by this guide are:

1. SCM for critical software for embedded systems
2. SCM for experimental development small system (prototype)
3. SCM for a software maintenance organization
4. SCM for a product line system

These type definitions hint at the optimal use of this document set. They are best used/ chosen when the objective is a single Software Configuration Management Plan for an organization or an installation. This contrasts with the choice of a standard which has the SCMP as a part of a project plan and, hence, a part of that specific project.

Table 11.2 provides a breakdown of the basic differences between these types, and somewhat on the various 'thought-processes' one should have in mind when choosing between them.

Table 11.2   SCM plan types

No.	Life-cycle control	Project size	SCM tools	Plan life span	Plan structure
1	Development	Medium	Advanced	Short	Structured
2	Concept	Small	Basic	Short	Informal
3	Operations	Large	On-line	Full	Structured
4	All	Small	Integrated	Full	Informal

It must be remembered, and indeed emphasized, that Software Configuration Management is both a service function and an integral part of the engineering process which creates software. It is a service to the client, the project's manager and quality assurance. At the same time, SCM is an inseparable part of the basic engineering process used to create and maintain software. This is true whether the SCM process is computerized or not — though clearly it is more useful when it is.

12

CONFIGURATION PLANNING FOR 'PROJECT' ORIENTED SCM

A Sample 'Project' Software Configuration Management Plan, based upon DoD-Std-2167A

document number:
QA-5901/MA3 for DID-MCCR-80030A

revision number

dates

Software Development Plan
for the
... CSCI ...
of ... system ...

contract number
CDRL Sequence Number

revision 0.2

prepared for:

prepared by:

authenticated by   approved by

(contracting agency)

(contractor)

date: date:

NOTES TO THE READER

This chapter serves as an example of a Software Development Plan written in accordance with a particular standard. Standards tend to describe overall structure of a document, but do not provide authors with analysis guidelines for discovering information needed for the creation of the document. Clearly, the emphasis of this example is upon Software Configuration Management. This chapter, as a part of the guidebook, is intended to provide these analysis tools. By mapping the information provided here with the idea presented by the other sections of the book, the reader will gain the broad picture needed by the myriad projects being implemented today.

This sample Software Development Plan is intended for a 'project' oriented development. Project does not necessarily imply product. Frequently (for example) many products may result from a specific project, or a project may intend to enhance an existing system. None the less, the work may be organized as a separate project. This author has seen many cases when a project was large enough to warrant opening a separate site or facility for it.

In cases such as these, a plan of this sort may very well be quite justified. The plan is intended to be used for only this project (while certainly it may be adopted for others, this is not the intention of its authors). It is not designed for the whole corporate environment (unless the whole corporation is only this project). That is the major reason for the incorporation of the SCMP as part of the Software Development Plan. For this type of environment, this type of plan is *very* suitable.

Documentation control
Index control
Document version no. 0.2

Revision no.	Index (Para. no.)	Date of update	New revision no.	New index (Para. no.)

Index and issue control list
Document version no. 0.2

Index #:									
Page no.:									
Update no:									
Date:									
Index #:									
Page no.:									
Update no:									
Date:									
Index #:									
Page no.:									
Update no:									
Date:									
Index #:									
Page no.:									
Update no:									
Date:									
Index #:									
Page no.:									
Update no:									
Date:									

CONTENTS

5 Formal qualification testing

5.1 Organization and resources — formal qualification testing
5.1.1 Organizational structure — formal qualification testing
5.1.2 Personnel — formal qualification testing
5.2 Test approach/philosophy
5.3 Test planning assumptions and constraints

6 Software product evaluations

6.1 Organization and resources — software product evaluations
6.1.1 Organizational structure — software product evaluations
6.1.2 Personnel — software product evaluations
6.2 Software product evaluations procedures and tools
6.2.1 Procedures
6.2.2 Tools
6.3 Subcontractor products
6.4 Software product evaluation records
6.5 Activity-dependent product evaluations

7 Software Configuration Management

7.1 Organization and resources — Configuration Management
7.1.1 Organizational structure — Configuration Management
7.1.2 Personnel — Configuration Management
7.2 Configuration identification
7.2.1 Developmental configuration identification
7.2.2 Identification methods
7.3 Configuration control
7.3.1 Flow of configuration control
7.3.2 Reporting documentation
7.3.3 Review procedures
7.3.4 Storage, handling and delivery of project media
7.3.5 Additional control
7.4 Configuration status accounting
7.5 Configuration audits
7.6 Preparation for specification authentication
7.7 Configuration management major milestones

8 Other software development functions

8.1 (function name)
8.1.1 Organizational structure — (function name)
8.1.2 Personnel — (function name)
8.1.3 Other resources — (function name)
8.1.4 Methods and procedures

9 Notes

9.1 Acronyms
9.2 Glossary of special terms

1 SCOPE

1.1 Identification

This document provides a description of the activities to be performed by [. . .] during the design, development, testing and maintenance of the [. . .], also referred to as [. . .]. n Computer Software Configuration Items (CSCIs) are being developed as part of this contract. This software development plan (SDP) applies to the following CSCIs:

1. [. . .]
2. [. . .]

1.2 System overview

All software — both deliverable and non-deliverable — for the [. . .] project is developed according to this formal software development plan. This software development is organized as a subcontracted project under the main project. The formal plan is written according to the United States Department of Defense Standard for Defense Systems DoD-Std-2167A, and the subsidiary Data Item Definition. (See Section 2.1, Military standard 13: DI-MCCR-80030A; 'Software Development Plan (SDP)'.)

It must be noted that this DID as defined supersedes DI-MCCR-80009 and DI-MCCR-80030. As such, these DIDs are not referenced in this SDP.

The Software Development Plan is constructed in accordance with the sections outlined by the chosen standard, and as they appear in Table 12.1.

Table 12.1   Structure of the Software Development Plan

1.	Scope
2.	Referenced Documents
3.	Software Development Management
4.	Software Engineering
5.	Formal Qualification Testing
6.	Software Product Evaluations
7.	Software Configuration Management

All software development activities are organized in accordance with this Software Development Plan. Sections 3.1 and 3.2 describe the methods of software project management used and milestoning for the various activities.

1.3 Document overview

This document serves two purposes:

1. The first purpose of this document is to provide the information necessary to guide project management of the [. . .], in the tasks involved in the development of the software for this module.
2. The second purpose of this document is to make all of the management tasks and management information visible to the whole audience of interested parties.

1.4 Relationship to other plans

This product development is organized with the aid of three managerial documentation plans:

1. The Software Development Plan (SDP) — this document
2. The Hardware Development Plan (HDP)
3. The Product Quality Assurance Plan (PAP)

These plans are independent of each other. Contained within this SDP are the Software Configuration Management (SCM) activities and Plans to be applied to the system and its CSCIs.

To ensure consistency, and for all contractual requirements, all configuration management change requests are reviewed, analysed and evaluated to assess their effects upon each approved configuration item.

2 APPLICABLE DOCUMENTS

2.1 Military standards

1. DoD-Std-2167A; 'Defense system software development'; 29 February 1988; United States Department of Defense.
2. DI-CMAN-80534; 'System/Segment Design Document (SSDD)'; 29 February 1988; United States Department of Defense.
3. DI-MCCR-80012A; 'Software Design Document (SDD)'; 29 February 1988; United States Department of Defense.
4. DI-MCCR-80014A; 'Software Test Plan (STP)'; 29 February 1988; United States Department of Defense.
5. DI-MCCR-80015A; 'Software Test Description (STD)'; 29 February 1988; United States Department of Defense.
6. DI-MCCR-80017A; 'Software Test Report (STR)'; 29 February 1988; United States Department of Defense.
7. DI-MCCR-80019A; 'Software User's Manual (SUM)'; 29 February 1988; United States Department of Defense.
8. DI-MCCR-80021A; 'Software Programmer's Manual (SPM)'; 29 February 1988; United States Department of Defense.
9. DI-MCCR-80025A; 'Software Requirements Specification (SRS)'; 29 February 1988; United States Department of Defense.
10. DI-MCCR-80026A; 'Interface Requirements Specification (IRS)'; 29 February 1988; United States Department of Defense.
11. DI-MCCR-80027A; 'Interface Design Document (IDD)'; 29 February 1988; United States Department of Defense.
12. DI-MCCR-80029A; 'Software Product Specification (SPS)'; 29 February 1988; United States Department of Defense.
13. DI-MCCR-80030A; 'Software Development Plan (SDP)'; 29 February 1988; United States Department of Defense.

14. MIL-HDBK-472; 'Maintainability Prediction'; 24 May 1966; Military Standardization Handbook.
15. MIL-Std-480A; 'Configuration Control — Engineering Changes, Deviations and Waivers'; 12 April 1978; Department of Defense.
16. MIL-Std-483; 'Configuration Management Practices for Systems, Equipment, Munitions and Computer Software'; 31 January 1985; Department of the Air Force.
17. MIL-Std-490A; 'Specification Practices'; 4 June 1985; Department of Defense.
18. MIL-Std-1388-1A; 'Logistic Support Analysis'; 11 April 1983; Department of Defense.
19. MIL-Std-1388-2A; 'DoD Requirements for a Logistic Support Analysis Record'; 20 July 1984; Department of Defense.
20. MIL-Std-1521 B; 'Technical reviews and audits for systems, equipments, and computer software'; 1 June 1976; Department of Defense.
21. MIL-Std-2155 (AS); 'Failure reporting, analysis and corrective action system'; 24 July 1985; Department of Defense.
22. MIL-M-85337; 'Manual, Requirements for quality assurance program'; Department of Defense.
23. MIL-N-18307; 'Nomenclature and identification for electronic, aeronautical and aeronautical support equipment'; Department of Defense.
24. MIL-H-46855B (2); 'Human engineering requirements for military systems, equipment and facilities'; amendment 2; 5 April 1984; Department of Defense.
25. DOD-Std-00100D; 'Engineering drawings and associated lists'; 3 April 1987; Department of Defense.
26. MIL-Std-970; 'Standards and specifications, order of preference for the selection of'; 1 October 1987; Department of Defense.

2.2   Other standards

1. ANSI/IEEE Std-729-1983; 'IEEE Standard Glossary of Software Engineering Terminology'; 18 February 1983; Institute of Electrical and Electronic Engineers.
2. ANSI/IEEE Std-610.2-1987; 'IEEE Standard Glossary of Computer Applications Terminology'; 29 May 1987; Institute of Electrical and Electronic Engineers.
3. IEEE Std-730.1-1989; 'IEEE Standard for Software Quality Assurance Plans'; 10 October 1989; Institute of Electrical and Electronic Engineers.
4. ANSI/IEEE Std-983-1986; 'IEEE Guide for Software Quality Assurance Planning'; 13 January 1986; Institute of Electrical and Electronic Engineers.
5. ANSI/IEEE Std-1008-1987; 'IEEE Standard for Software Unit Testing'; 29 December 1986; Institute of Electrical and Electronic Engineers.
6. IEEE Std-828-1983; 'IEEE Standard for Software Configuration Management Plans'; Institute of Electrical and Electronic Engineers.

TBD — To Be Defined.

2.3   Other documents

TBD.

[*This section is 'project' and organization oriented.*]

3 SOFTWARE DEVELOPMENT MANAGEMENT

3.1 Project organization and resources

3.1.1 Contractor facilities

Contractor facilities consist of both hardware and software items which are acquired for this development. The hardware items are defined by paragraph 3.1.1.1, the software items by paragraph 3.1.1.2.

3.1.1.1 Hardware items acquired for this development
All of the following hardware items (at least) are acquired for the purposes of this software development, and are used to both perform the basic development tasks and to enhance the efficiency of the software professionals performing the development functions.

The development environment consists of the following hardware components:

1. Personal computer (industry compatible)
    TBD.
2. Software: (see 3.1.1.2 [2])
    TBD.
3. Additional hardware items
    TBD.

3.1.1.2 Software items acquired for this development
All of the following software items (at least) are acquired for the purposes of this software development, and are used to enhance the efficiency of the software professionals performing the development functions.

The development environment consists of the following software components:

1. PC operating system
   MSDOS
2. Design and code development code editor
   TBD.
3. Prototype of the user environment (man–machine interface), an in-house development of TBD Corporation
4. Word processor package
   'WordPerfect 5.0'

3.1.1.3 The pseudo-target environment for testing
    TBD.

3.1.2 Government furnished equipment

    TBD.

3.1.3 Organizational structure

The software for the [. . .] is organized as a subproject of the project which develops the [. . .]. This is a subsystem of the [. . .] as developed by [. . .].

The actual software (program) development is carried out by three computer software specialists (for parts of the development two programmers may be sufficient, depending upon actual needs) and a software team leader (STL). The software team leader reports directly to the project manager.

There exist direct (non-hierarchical) links between the software team and both the quality assurance and documentation teams (see Fig. 12.1 for a graphical representation of these relationships). The addition of the quality assurance (see Section 6 of this Software Development Plan) documentation (see the Documentation Plan for the project; ref. paragraph 2.3) and Configuration Management (see Section 7 of this Software Development Plan) functionality provides additional manpower which supports the software team development effort.

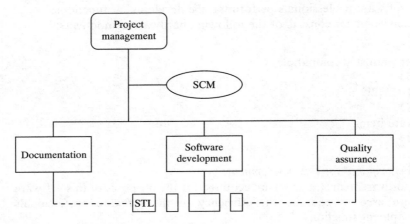

Figure 12.1 Software team interrelationships

3.1.4 The software project team

The software project team consists of four software professionals (as stated above). The following paragraphs depict their experience and credentials.

Lead Programmer
Education: M.Sc. (1986) in computer science from . . .
Development environments: VAX/VMS, MS-DOS, XENIX, AIX, OS/2, UNIX (system 5 and Berkeley)
Languages: C, FORTRAN, Pascal, Basic, Ada (courses)
Experience: . . . years of professional experience, in all of the following areas:
Engineering of personal computer tools — an application generator environment, word processor, a text-based information retrieval system.
Numerous conversions of software packages/products from one system to another.
Computer graphics with simulation.
Geodesic information retrieval systems.
Interests: Owner of a private pilot's licence.

Programmer 2:
Education: B.Sc. in general engineering from . . .
Development environments: VAX/VMS, MS-DOS, UNIX (system 5 and Berkeley).
Languages: C, FORTRAN, Ada.
Experience: A total of . . . years of software experience, in all of the following areas: . . . years of experience developing in Ada for the United States Army, solid state and steady state analysis programming, application generator, managed a computer centre for a major academic institution.

Programmer 3:
Education: High school
Development environments: PC and MS-DOS, IBM Mainframe (30xx, 43xx, S/3x), Data General.
Languages: C, Basic, Pascal.
Experience: A total of . . . years of software experience, development of communications systems, application generators, specialized computerized controllers, real time systems.

3.2   Schedule and milestones

3.2.1 Development, major activities

This project, like any software development project, divides into: activities (labelled An, where 'n' is a sequential number), events (labelled En, where 'n' is a sequential number), deliverables, requirements (read: prerequisites, labelled Rn, where 'n' is a sequential number) and baselines. This paragraph, with its subsections, describes the activities, events and requirements. Baselines are described in Section 7 of this SDP. Deliverables are described by the Documentation plan of the project (see 2.3).

3.2.1.1   Activities

3.2.1.1.1 EACH ACTIVITY HAS THE FOLLOWING ASPECTS:

- Activity code (for Gantt charting, etc.)
- Activity name
- Start date
- Target completion date
- Dependencies (upon other activities and/or requirements and/or events)
- Description
- Risks
- Deliverables

TBD.

3.2.1.1.2 CONTRACT BACKGROUND DOCUMENT PREPARATION

Activity code	A1
Start date	TBD
Target completion date	TBD
Dependencies	none
Description	TBD
Risks	none
Deliverables	TBD

3.2.1.1.3 PROTOTYPE PREPARATION

Activity code	A2
Start date	TBD
Target completion date	TBD
Dependencies	none
Description	TBD
Risks	none
Deliverables	TBD

3.2.1.1.4 SOFTWARE REQUIREMENTS SPECIFICATION (SRS)

Activity code	A3
Start date	TBD
Target completion date	TBD
Dependencies	none
Description	TBD
Risks	none
Deliverables	TBD

3.2.1.1.5 . . . DIALOG MANAGER/GUI

Activity code	A4
Start date	TBD
Target completion date	TBD
Dependencies	none
Description	TBD
Risks	none
Deliverables	TBD

3.2.1.1.6 INTERNAL LOGIC DEVELOPMENT

Activity code	A5
Start date	TBD
Target completion date	TBD
Dependencies	none
Description	TBD
Risks	none
Deliverables	TBD

3.2.1.1.7 . . . GENERATION

Activity code	A6
Start date	TBD
Target completion date	TBD
Dependencies	none
Description	TBD
Risks	none
Deliverables	TBD

3.2.1.1.8 INTERFACE PREPARATION

Activity code	A7
Start date	TBD
Target completion date	TBD
Dependencies	none
Description	TBD
Risks	none
Deliverables	TBD

3.2.1.1.9 INITIAL INTEGRATION

Activity code	A8
Start date	TBD
Target completion date	TBD
Dependencies	none
Description	TBD
Risks	none
Deliverables	TBD

3.2.1.1.10 FINAL INTEGRATION

Activity code	A20
Start date	TBD
Target completion date	TBD
Dependencies	none
Description	TBD
Risks	none
Deliverables	TBD

3.2.1.2 Prerequisite requirements for the development activities
. . . items have been defined as being prerequisite to the success of this development. Success, in this sense, refers to: 'on time and within budget'! That means that there are six external events — events over which no control exists within the development project — which must be completed on time for the contractual completion of this development.

3.2.1.2.1 REMOTE UNIT

Requirement code	R1
Target date	TBD
Description	TBD

3.2.1.2.2 PROTOTYPE APPROVAL

Requirement code	R2
Target date	TBD
Description	TBD

3.2.1.2.3 HARDWARE SPECIFICATIONS

Requirement code	R3
Target date	TBD
Description	TBD

3.2.1.2.4 PERIPHERALS DELIVERY

Requirement code	R4
Target date	TBD
Description	TBD

3.2.1.2.5 . . .

Requirement code	R5
Target date	TBD
Description	TBD

3.2.1.2.6 FULL INTERFACE SPECIFICATIONS

Requirement code	R6
Target date	TBD
Description	TBD

3.2.1.3   Events

Nine significant events need to occur in the development of this project. The following paragraphs briefly describe each one.

3.2.1.3.1 PROJECT START

Event code	E1
Target date	TBD
Description	TBD

3.2.1.3.2 CONTRACT SIGNATURE

Event code	E2
Target date	TBD
Description	Contract signature

3.2.1.3.3 SOFTWARE REQUIREMENTS REVIEW

Event code	E3
Target date	TBD
Description	A client review for all software requirements, including: software requirements specifications, draft test plan, product assurance plan

3.2.1.3.4 PRELIMINARY DESIGN REVIEW

Event code	E4
Target date	TBD
Description	An in-house review for the high-level design documents, and including also: corrected requirements, test plan, draft acceptance test procedure, test design specifications

3.2.1.3.5 CRITICAL DESIGN REVIEW

Event code	E5
Target date	TBD
Description	A client review for detailed design, and including also: corrected requirements and high-level design documents, test procedures, and updated test design

3.2.1.3.6 START SOFTWARE/SOFTWARE AND SOFTWARE/HARDWARE INTEGRATION

Event code	E6
Target date	TBD
Description	Integration start

3.2.1.3.7 TEST REVIEW

Event code	E7
Target date	TBD
Description	An in-house review for establishing test readiness, and including also: unit test results, test design (re-review), test procedures (re-review) and (perhaps) source code

3.2.1.3.8 DELIVERY

Event code	E8
Target date	TBD
Description	All software and related documentation is delivered for client approval

3.2.1.3.9 ACCEPTANCE TEST PROCEDURE

Event code	E9
Target date	TBD
Description	Final project approval

3.2.2 *Activity network*

The essential aspects of this paragraph are included with the information for paragraph 3.2.1 (dependencies for development activities). The important aspect of the activity network is the element of time restrictions. The management of the software for this project has examined this question very carefully, and is continuing to do so. It is estimated that an average of 2.5–3 staff programmers are needed for accomplishing the development. However, to ensure delivery on schedule in the event of unforeseen difficulties, the staff has been expanded to include three full-time staff plus program management.

3.2.3 Source identification

Sources of all resources needed for this development have been included in the information of paragraph 3.2.1, along with a plan for resource acquisition. Refer to the project Gantt chart for a pictorial representation.

3.3   Risk management

The risk management techniques used for this project are systematic and have been thoroughly tested by the methodology vendor. Four areas of risk have been perceived as associated with this development:

- Incorrect choice of development techniques is usually the largest risk in time/delivery critical projects. The proper choice of development techniques and the criticality of this function demand constant tuning and adaptation of these questions as the project progresses.
- The use of the chosen language (. . .) is still relatively new: truly experienced programmers are difficult to find. This potential hazard is addressed by utilization of programmers who have had some prior experience with the programming language, and also with the aid, whenever necessary, of a consultant with experience in the language.
- The target environment differs from the development environment. This may cause integration difficulties. This potential hazard is addressed by use of similar computing facilities to the target host during development.
- Non-delivery of the prerequisites on time.

3.4   Security

This project has no security requirements at this time.

3.5   Interface with associate contractors

The CSCIs identified by Section 1 interface with [. . .]. Their interfaces are defined in the interface requirements specification (IRS) and the appropriate interface design description (IDD) documents. These documents are prepared jointly by the appropriate representatives from each contractor.

Upon completion, the IRS document is submitted to software quality assurance for formal verification and validation (V&V). When all V&V cycles have completed, the IRS is then submitted as part of the allocated baseline to the [. . .] for authentication. After authentication, requests to change the IRS are coordinated by the affected contractors via their respective Change Control Boards (CCBs). All change requests are submitted for impact analysis before any further change activities may occur. All change requests are processed in accordance with procedures described in Section 7.3 of this SDP.

Preliminary IDDs are delivered to the contracting agency, upon completion of preliminary design work, only after having passed a process of software quality assurance (SQA) V&V. At time of submittal, IDD documents are placed under contractor configuration control. Modifications are reviewed by each contractor's CCB prior to incorporation into the updated IDD. The final IDD documents are submitted at the end of detailed design. All changes are reviewed and processed in accordance with Section 7.3 of this SDP.

3.6   Interface with software IV&V agent

No interface is foreseen, at this point, with independent verification and validation subcontractors for this development.

3.7   Subcontractor management

Part of this development is being produced by subcontractors [. . .], [. . .] and [. . .]. SCM and SQA requirements flow down to these subcontractors, with the appropriate changes (to reflect their developments).

All subcontractors supply software development plans, including SCM and SQA for evaluation and approval. Any updates or changes to these plans may be made only with the approval of the contracting agency.

Receiving inspections are conducted for all subcontractor developed and supplied software items. These inspections always include (at least):

1. All physical items are present.
2. Delivered software media have all been labelled properly.
3. The delivered software functions in accordance with the contractual requirements.
4. Delivered software code agrees with the documentation supplied.

Checklist 12.1

- Have all needed safeguards for the correct coordination of the contractor with project subcontractors been constructed?
- Can this coordination be clearly verified, as defined?

3.8   Formal reviews

3.8.1 Review outlines

Five formal reviews are designed for this development. As described in paragraph 3.2.1, these reviews are either client reviews or in-house. Paragraph 3.8.2 describes the client reviews. Paragraph 3.8.3 describes the in-house reviews.

3.8.2 Client reviews

1. Software requirements review
   Target date: TBD
   Review content:
   (a) Software requirements specifications
   (b) Draft test plan
   (c) Product assurance plan
2. Critical design review
   Target date: TBD
   Review content:
   (a) Detailed design
   (b) Corrected requirements and high-level design documents
   (c) Test procedures
   (d) Updated test design
3. Acceptance test procedure
   Target date: TBD
   Review content:
   (a) All documentation which may have needed to be updated
   (b) Final test results

3.8.3 In-house reviews

1. Preliminary design review
   Target date: TBD
   Review content:
   (a) High-level design documents
   (b) Corrected requirements
   (c) Test Plan
   (d) Draft acceptance test procedure
   (e) Test design specifications
2. Test Review
   Target date: TBD
   Review content:
   (a) Establish test readiness
   (b) Unit test results
   (c) Test design (re-review)
   (d) Test procedures (re-review)
   (e) Source code (if necessary)

3.9   Software development library

Software development libraries (SDL) are established to store and limit access to controlled software, documentation, tools and procedures used to facilitate the orderly development and subsequent support of project software. To more effectively control the system software as it is being developed, the SDLs are separated into three sets of libraries, each in its own domain. These library domains are: development, integration and testing and production.

The development SDL is used by project developers to generate software code and documentation, both new and updates. Individual programmers or programming teams are responsible for controlling their own computer software units (CSUs) and computer software components (CSCs) prior to submittal for SQA and integration and testing (I&T). The PVCS family of products, purchased from the INTERSOLV Corporation, are used for this control activity. The items purchased from them, and adapted to our uses, are as follows:

1. Version Manager (VM) — to control and record changes to project code and documentation. All programmer version control activities are performed automatically, in the 'background', by the SCM system software
2. Configuration Builder — to consistently build and rebuild systems and subsystems
3. Programmer's workbench 'PPE' — to provide for a consistent programming environment and a smooth interface to the other tools
4. Production Gateway (for coordination of SCM activities with various environments)

All software and related documentation is transferred to the I&T domain upon completion of the CSU testing. The I&T library domain is under the managerial control of [. . .]. The PVCS family of products are used for all configuration control activities performed by [. . .]. This includes object code, as well as source code. Clearly, while the Configuration Builder tool is certainly used by the developers, CB is the primary tool to be used by the I&T function. I&T is responsible for the maintenance of the makefiles.

The project librarian releases code for testing in a controlled manner. Using the PVCS security features, access lists are maintained by the SCM coordinator. All project librarians have read-only access. Read/write access is granted to programmers on a 'need-to-use' basis. Problems discovered during testing are recorded in the problem recording system database. This database interfaces with the SCM database via the SQL facility.

The production library domain contains master copies of all software and documentation which has been tested and integrated. Both deliverable and non-deliverable software is controlled by the production domain. This domain is also controlled via the PVCS toolset.

Checklist 12.2

- Has a procedure been constructed for the management, implementation, development and control of the software development library/libraries?
- Does this procedure include all steps necessary for both the code and the documentation?
- Does this paragraph of the plan describe the contractor's procedures or provide a reference to the document which does?
- Have access procedures to the SDL been established and documented?

3.10   Corrective action process

Problems detected in software and/or documentation are reported via the software problem report. These reports are recorded in the problem recording system by the librarian of the highest domain responsible for the component. The SPR identifies all information detected concerning the problem, the originator of the SPR, items affected, change categories and priorities. After recording, the librarian is responsible for bringing the SPR to the attention of the appropriate CCB for analysis, review and processing.

Actual changes to software and/or documentation are made to copies of the configuration items withdrawn from the SCM database via the PVCS GET command, with a LOCK on the particular revision of the logfile. All change activities are cross-referenced to the problem reporting system database. This cross-referencing allows the CCB to keep track of all change activity.

If an SPR is closed without a change being made to the software, the originator of the SPR is notified of the reasons.

3.11 Problem/change report

All problem reports and/or request for changes affecting SCM controlled items, are recorded via the software problem reporting system and the PVCS databases.

Checklist 12.3

- Has a formal procedure been established defining the format of formal problem/change reports?
- Has a formal procedure been established defining the methodology of formal problem/change reports?
- Has a formal procedure been established defining the documentation of formal problem/change reports?
- Has a formal procedure been established defining the corrective action resulting from formal problem/change reports?
- Does the formal change/problem report include, at least, all of the following information:
  - system/project name
  - originator
  - problem number
  - problem name
  - software element(s) affected
  - document(s) affected
  - origination date
  - category and priority
  - description of problem
  - analyst
  - date assigned
  - date completed;
  - recommended solution
  - impacts
  - problem status
  - approval of solution
  - follow-up action

- corrector
- correction date
- version number
- correction time
- implementation solution

---

4 SOFTWARE ENGINEERING

4.1 Organization and resources — software engineering

4.1.1 Organizational structure — software engineering

In this software development, a single project team of four people is sufficient. This organization (software development team) is organized as displayed by paragraph 3.1.4. This team is responsible for all software development activities and all software engineering activities. The software engineering activities do not include quality assurance.

4.1.2 Personnel — software engineering

This paragraph is not relevant to this SDP. See paragraph 3.1.4.

4.1.3 Software engineering environment

4.1.3.1 Software items
TBD.
[*This section is 'project' and organization oriented.*]

4.1.3.2 Hardware and firmware items
TBD.
[*This section is 'project' and organization oriented.*]

4.1.3.3 Proprietary nature and government rights
TBD.

4.1.3.4 Installation, control and maintenance
TBD.
[*This section is 'project' and organization oriented.*]

4.2 Software standards and procedures

4.2.1 Software development techniques and methodologies

4.2.1.1 Software requirements analysis
All software requirements specifications are created as formal documents with the aid of a software package intended for that purpose.

The requirements analysis specifications are presented in a 'graphic syntax', using a standard, industry compatible methodology known as Ward/Mellor data flow diagrams (references are not a part of this SDP). This methodology is designed for embedded computer systems, and consists of:

- Modified Yourdon/DeMarco data flow diagrams
- Booch diagrams (OODS)
- Entity/relationship diagrams
- State diagrams

Use of this methodology allows the maximum advantages of data flow technologies and structured analysis, without losing the benefits of object-oriented analysis, customarily used with the Ada language.

The diagrams are then augmented with textual explanations and computer-generated analysis reports.

4.2.1.2 Preliminary design and detailed design
All design aspects of this development are performed using the Ward/Mellor design methodology (data flow diagrams, state diagrams, and/or entity diagrams, as needed), and utilizing the design tools.

4.2.1.3 Coding and CSU testing
All code developed for this project is written in the Ada programming language, according to ANSI/MIL-Std-1815A-1983; *Reference Manual for the Ada Programming Language*.

4.2.1.4 CSC integration and testing
The testing of the deliverable software is performed in three stages:

1. The software is tested in the development environment (PC-386).
2. The software is integrated (initial software/software integration) and tested.
3. The final integration is performed on the target system.

4.2.1.5 CSCI testing
Final integration and CSCI testing is performed on the target system. This testing is performed in the operational environment and in conjunction with the console.

4.2.2 Software development files

In this software development, the software development team is responsible for all software development activities and all software development files and libraries. Software development files are maintained with the aid of PVCS.

4.2.3 Design standards

The design standards to be used are purchased standards. These standards have been tried and used in several environments for embedded systems, and are compatible with those of DoD-Std-2167A.

4.2.4   *Coding standards*

The design standards to be used are purchased standards. These standards have been tried and used in several environments for embedded systems, and are compatible with those of DOD-STD-2167A.

4.3 Non-developmental software

Not relevant to this software development.

> [*Clearly, this section is very much dependent upon the specific orientation of the project and the organization.*]

5 FORMAL QUALIFICATION TESTING

5.1   Organization and resources — formal qualification testing

5.1.1 *Organizational structure — formal qualification testing*

All formal qualification testing is performed by a special testing group formed by final integration of all CSCIs with the HWCIs.

5.1.2 *Personnel — formal qualification testing*

Not relevant at this time.

> [*This section is 'project' and organization oriented.*]

5.2   Test approach/philosophy

To be defined by the formal testing documents (see Section 2.1 [4, 5, 6]):

- DI-MCCR-80014A; 'Software Test Plan (STP)'; 29 February 1988; United States Department of Defense.
- DI-MCCR-80015A; 'Software Test Description (STD)'; 29 February 1988; United States Department of Defense.
- DI-MCCR-80017A; 'Software Test Report (STR)'; 29 February 1988; United States Department of Defense.

5.3   Test planning assumptions and constraints

Defined by the formal test documentation.

> [*This section is 'project' and organization oriented.*]

6 SOFTWARE PRODUCT EVALUATIONS

6.1 Organization and resources — software product evaluations

6.1.1 Organizational structure — software product evaluations

TBD.

[This section is 'project' and organization oriented. Care should be taken to give this section real meaning, and not provide 'lip-service'.]

6.1.2 Personnel — software product evaluations

TBD.

[This section is 'project' and organization oriented. Care should be taken to give this section real meaning, and not provide 'lip-service'.]

6.2 Software product evaluations procedures and tools

6.2.1 Procedures

TBD.

[This section is 'project' and organization oriented. Care should be taken to give this section real meaning, and not provide 'lip-service'.]

6.2.2 Tools

TBD.

[This section is 'project' and application oriented. Care should be taken to give this section real meaning, and not provide 'lip-service'.]

6.3 Subcontractor products

TBD.

[This section is 'project' and organization oriented. Care should be taken to give this section real meaning, and not provide 'lip-service'.]

6.4 Software product evaluation records

TBD.

6.5 Activity-dependent product evaluations

TBD.

7 SOFTWARE CONFIGURATION MANAGEMENT

7.1 Organization and resources — configuration management

7.1.1 Organizational structure — configuration management

SCM for this project is designed to respond to rapid system modification needs, both during initial development and during the later maintenance stages of the system life-cycle. During design and development, the project manager has full responsibility for all project management functions, including SCM. During this period of the life-cycle, the project manager and/or the PM delegate has full authority for any changes to any configuration item (CSU, CSC or CSCI). However, while full authority rests with the PM, all change activities must be documented by being performed via the services of the PVCS family of tools.

In addition to their development duties, staff from the developing organization supports project SCM by complying with procedures defined in this plan and conferring with the project manager on changes affecting their responsibilities. The coordinator of SCM activities provides assistance to these activities, upon request.

Changes which affect approved baselines must be approved by the CCB prior to submittal for customer approval. The CCB has sole responsibility for priorities and schedules for all change requests. The project manager is the CCB chair.

Checklist 12.4

- Has each and every aspect of the contractor's organization which deals with the Configuration Management of the project's software been described?
- Is this description accompanied with a graphic diagram?
- Have the Software Configuration Management related responsibilities of each part of the organization been specified, including interrelationships?
- Do these interrelationships include interfacing with the testing and QA organizations?
- Does the description of each organization include resources and personnel?

7.1.2 Personnel — configuration management

TBD.

[*This section is 'project' and organization oriented. Care should be taken to give this section real meaning, and not provide 'lip-service'.*]

7.2 Configuration identification

7.2.1 Developmental configuration identification

Baselines are periodically established for the control of the configurations of the CSCIs. The following baselines are defined as minimal (additional baselines may be established at the discretion of the project manager):

1. Functional baseline — all system specifications.

2. Allocated baseline — software and interface requirements specifications.
3. Product baseline — software product specifications.

All documents which form a part of each baseline are placed under formal configuration control, in the product domain, via the PVCS control mechanisms, after SQA V&V and customer authorization.

The developmental configuration of each CSCI is based upon the formal software design document (SDD). The CSCI SDD is assigned a formal identification code by [. . .] at the start of its development and stored in the SDL appropriate to its development before submittal to SQA for verification. All changes are documented via PVCS facilities.

At the completion of the coding and CSU testing stages, all items (code, test documentation and updated SDD) are assigned new identification numbers and version number and transferred to the I&T domain. PVCS facilities are used to maintain all members of the I&T domain. After successful I&T each CSC is transferred to the product domain. PVCS facilities are used to maintain all members of the product domain.

7.2.2   Identification methods

All CSCIs, CSCs, CSUs and documentation produced by this contract are identified according to the methods detailed in [. . .]. CSCs, CSUs and document files are numbered automatically by the PVCS facilities. All CSCI version identifiers are embedded within the PVCS database before any use.

7.3   Configuration control

7.3.1 Flow of configuration control

All requests for change to any baselined item must be submitted to the Change Control Board for approval. All such requests must be submitted upon the corporate forms designed for this purpose.

Due to the nature of this project, the project manager has complete authority for approval/disapproval, reviewing, categorizing and prioritizing of all change requests to nonbaselined items. On baselined items, the project manager must be consulted for any work or rework which may adversely affect the schedule. Records are retained for a period of (at least) three years concerning all change requests which have been rejected and five years concerning all change requests which have been implemented. Change requests which may affect both hardware and software must be approved by the customer before scheduling.

7.3.2 Reporting documentation

7.3.2.1   Engineering change proposals
ECPs are used for recording change requests to the systems' functional, allocated and/or product baselines configuration identifications. (After delivery, maintenance, perfectory, corrective or preventive, forms various product baselines.) This project uses the ECP form taken from DD Form 1692, prepared in accordance with MIL-STD-480B.

7.3.2.2   Specification change notices
TBD.

7.3.3 Review procedures

7.3.3.1 Configuration Control Board procedures
The CCB is chaired by the project manager. The CCB secretary is the SCM coordinator. The CCB's defined purposes are as follows:

1. Establish the necessity and justifications for the requested change.
2. Obtain an adequate specification of the requested change for purpose of understanding ramifications, scope and impact of the change upon other aspects of the project (expressly INCLUSIVE of timetable).
3. Develop estimates for the costs of the change:
   (a) cost of evaluation
   (b) cost of implementation
   (c) documentation
   (d) other costs, direct or implied
4. Assign change classification and priorities.

CCB meeting minutes are recorded and filed within PVCS as part of the project documentation database.

7.3.4 Storage, handling and delivery of project media

All controlled software (program files, documentation, procedures, makefiles, etc.) are maintained in the SDLs.

Working copies are always deposited in the development domain SDL. All information contained in the I&T domain is limited to read-only access for all personnel other than the integration coordinator and the SCM coordinator.

Master copies of all CSCIs, including (at least) programs, makefiles, documentation and all other parts, are retained within the production domain. Everything in the production domain is maintained as read-only for all access other than the SCM coordinator. Only the SCM coordinator is permitted to make copies of CSCIs (or parts thereof) for delivery to the customer. Copies of all items are submitted to the customer in accordance with the contract data requirement list (CDRL).

Access to all proprietary software, including documentation, is on a need-to-know basis. To authorize access, the project manager or the customer delegate must submit a memo to the SCM coordinator, with a copy to the SQA coordinator, identifying those permitted specific access authorization. The SCM coordinator defines the PVCS access database in accordance with this memo *only*.

7.3.5 Additional control

None.

7.4 Configuration status accounting

Configuration status accounting consists of maintaining records which denote the status of configuration items and documents and the implementation of approved changes to controlled items. This information is used to compile reports which are used for the managing of the project and for the CDRL. This project maintains the following types of reports and records:

1. *Status of software problems and software change requests.* Status reports of all PRs and/ or CRs are prepared for management. These reports identify the PR/CR, its purpose, items affected, current status and assigned responsibilities.
2. *Status of engineering change proposals.* ECP status records are maintained by the SCM coordinator in the residual database maintained alongside the PVCS database. ECP records contain the ECP number, submission date, title, description, originator (name, title, telephone code), documents affected. As documents are revised, a cross reference is maintained showing which ECPs affected which documents and which documents affected each ECP (incorporation).
3. *Status of specification change notices.* The SCM coordinator maintains records on the status of each change to a specification. These records include: SCN number, originator (name, title, telephone code), documents affected, submittal date, cross-reference to ECPs and/or CRs. As SCNs are incorporated into a specification document, SCN status records are updated to show present status.
4. *Record of revision number changes.* PVCS is used to keep track of the actual changes between each software and document revision. This information is exported (via the VSQL facility) for the updating of the records listed above as '1', '2', and '3'.
5. *Version description document.* Upon establishment of the first product baseline, a VDD is developed and maintained for each deliverable CSCI. The VDD lists all computer software and documentation comprising the current version, makefiles needed for the configuration build activity, operational instructions (load, operate and install), equipment needed and identification numbers of media and documentation.

As changes occur, the VDDs are updated to reflect new versions and interim releases. PVCS is used to generate lists of the program units (files, modules, etc.) and documentation of which the CSCI is comprised.

VDDs are prepared by the SCM coordinator in accordance with DI-MCCR-80013A.

7.5 Configuration audits

Physical and functional audits are conducted for all deliverable software items — in accordance with section 3, paragraph 3.2.1. All audits are conducted in accordance with MIL-STD-1521B. All such audits are chaired by the SQA coordinator. The audit is co-chaired by the Software Configuration Management coordinator and a customer representative.

A functional configuration audit (FCA) is conducted on each computer software configuration item to validate the satisfactory completion of all defined development tasks and that the CSCI has achieved the required functional and performance characteristics. Formal test plans, designs and procedures are compared to official test data. All results are checked for accuracy and completeness.

Audits of software test reports are performed to validate accurate and complete reporting of development results.

All software releases must be regression tested to ensure accuracy of the change implementation and continued integrity of the CSCI.

All updates to baselined documents are audited by the SQA function to ensure accuracy and continued integrity of the documentation set.

All approved ECPs and/or SCNs are audited upon incorporation to ensure accuracy and integrity of the documentation set.

Any audit deficiencies are incorporated in the audit result report. Follow through techniques on correcting discovered anomalies shall be at the discretion of the SQA coordinator.

Physical examination of each CSCI is made ('white-box' analysis) to verify that all software 'as-coded' conforms to the technical specifications. At the time of the physical configuration audit (PCA) the SCM coordinator assembles and makes available all data concerning the CSCI. Project status accounting records are used to help compile this information. This must include, at least, the updated set of listings and the final draft of the baseline specifications.

Customer acceptance of the CSCIs and the product specifications are provided in writing to the project manager. In the event of a customer's rejection of a CSCI or part thereof, the customer should include full reasons for the rejection.

7.6   Preparation for specification authentication

7.6.1 Submitting specifications for review

CSCI specifications are submitted to the [. . .] in accordance with CDRL requirements. Specification documents are prepared for submittal by the SCM coordinator, after SQA audit and review and submitted through the project manager.

Upon receipt [. . .] reviews the specification documents for acceptability. Lack of an answer within 15 days is considered agreement with specification contents. All items of concern or perceived anomalies are submitted back to the project manager for reaction. Upon resolution of all anomalies, the specification is accepted as authenticated and baselined.

7.6.2 Ensuring incorporation of approved changes

Once authenticated, any requested changes are recorded on SCNs and submitted to the customer for acceptance. The contractor modifies specification only after SCN approval. The SCM coordinator is responsible for maintaining the VDD documents.

7.7   Configuration management major milestones

TBD.

[This section is very 'project' oriented. Care should be taken to give this section real meaning, and not provide 'lip-service'.]

8.   OTHER SOFTWARE DEVELOPMENT FUNCTIONS

[This section of the plan is used only if there are 'other' such functions. Otherwise, this section may be eliminated.]

8.1 (function name)

8.1.1 Organizational structure — (function name)

TBD.

8.1.2 Personnel — (function name)

TBD.

8.1.3 Other resources — (function name)

TBD.

8.1.4 Methods and procedures

TBD.

9. NOTES

9.1 Acronyms

This section does not include a glossary of terms, as the actual glossary is adopted from that of the whole book. (In a 'real' plan, of course, this section would contain such a list.)

9.2 Glossary of special terms

This section does not include a glossary of terms, as the actual glossary is adopted from that of the whole book. (In a 'real' plan, of course, this section would contain such a list.)

13

CONFIGURATION PLANNING FOR A 'CORPORATE-WIDE' ENVIRONMENT

**A sample 'corporate-wide'
Software Configuration Management
Plan, based upon IEEE Standard 828**

Software Configuration Management Plan for Critical Software for Embedded Systems

M. Ben-Menachem
Quality Awareness Ltd
P.O. Box 10268
Ramat-Gans 52100
ISRAEL

23 August 1993
version 0.3

COPYRIGHT

NOTICE OF DISCLAIMER

NOTES TO THE READER

This chapter serves as an example of a Software Configuration Management Plan written in accordance with a specific standard: 'IEEE Standard for Software Configuration Management Plans, ANSI/IEEE Std-828-1983'. This document is a recognized American National Standard and is being considered for adoption as a standard by the International Standards Organization (ISO). The standard was produced by a working group of the IEEE (Software Engineering Subcommittee — this author has been a member of this committee and the working group since before the first version was created).

Actually, to be more specific, this particular example is based upon both this standard and another IEEE-produced document. There is a document which is called the: 'IEEE Guide to Software Configuration Management' (also an American National Standard). This Guide was written as an accompanying document to the standard (the previous version, 828-1983) and augments the information in it. It is noteworthy that this Guide is much less tightly coupled with the newer version of the standard, from 1990. This is unfortunate. This document (the Guide) is highly recommended to the reader who is genuinely interested in understanding as much as possible about SCM. As a public document, this Guide is probably one of the best documents of its kind.

In particular, in this chapter we have drawn from the following Appendices to the standard: *Appendix A: Software Configuration Management Plan for Critical Software for Embedded Systems*; *Appendix B: Software Configuration Management Plan for Experimental Development Small Systems*; *Appendix C: Software Configuration Management Plan for a Software Maintenance Organization*; *Appendix D: Configuration Management Plan for a Product Line System*.

It is very likely that in your organization none of these Appendices is exactly what is needed. There is nothing wrong with creating an amalgamation of them. In this chapter, while the 'main line' deals with 'critical software', we shall try to suggest pointers which may help to implement this kind of a plan for other kinds of situations.

As in most standards, this one (ANSI/IEEE Std-828-1983) tends to emphasis the intended overall structure of the document to be produced (the SCM Plan). No analysis guidelines are provided for information needed to create the document. This chapter, as a part of the guidebook, is intended to alleviate this lack.

By the mapping of the information provided here, with ideas presented by other sections of the book, the reader will be provided with the broad picture needed by the myriad projects being implemented today. Keep in mind that this type of plan is designed for a broad 'corporate' plan, rather than the project specific plan. There are critical differences. See the previous two chapters for a better understanding of what these differences are and what they may mean to your organization.

In addition, many of the specific paragraphs of this chapter are highlighted with an arrowhead to help in the adaptation of their information for other set-up needs.

Documentation control
Index control
Document version no. 0.3

Revision no.	Index (Para. no.)	Date of update	New revision no.	New index no.

CONTENTS

1 INTRODUCTION

1.1 Purpose of the SCM Plan

The purpose of this document is to plan all Software Configuration Management (SCM) activities for the [. . .] corporation, as defined by project specifications and other documents described for projects, by contracts. This Plan also documents the activities and directives for management support of the project. This Software Configuration Management Plan (SCMP) is subordinate to the project Software Quality Assurance Plan (SQAP) and the Software Development Plan (SDP).

▶ **For prototype systems:**
   The paragraph places its central concept around the capture of critical information which will be needed for future releases of the final, target system.

▶ **For the maintenance project:**
   This paragraph should place all emphasis upon questions involving processes of change control and enhancement releases.

▶ **For the product line systems:**
   This paragraph should emphasize the maintenance processes during the period that the product is being sold/marketed. Also, enhancement and corrective releases must be controlled.

1.2 Scope

The scope of this SCMP is defined by the SDP of the project, to which this plan is subordinate.
   [*Note: This section defines exactly which 'items' this Plan is meant to manage!*]

▶ **For prototype systems:**
   The paragraph lists each item and item type of the final, target system.

▶ **For the maintenance project:**
   It is very important to remember that there may be special, perhaps even non-deliverable, software items which must be maintained, such as test scripts and simulators.

▶ **For the product line systems:**
   This paragraph discusses the needs created by different types of software (e.g. a database of information in COBOL, an EEPROMed program for special equipment at the customer site and a special GUI MMI for the end-user).

1.3 Definitions and mnemonics

1.3.1 Definitions

TBD — To Be Defined.

1.3.2 *Mnemonics*

TBD.

1.4 References

IEEE Standards:
1. IEEE Std-828-1983; 'Standard for Software Configuration Management Plans'.
2. IEEE Std-828-1990; 'Standard for Software Configuration Management Plans'.
3. ANSI/IEEE Std-1042-1987; 'Guide to Software Configuration Management'.

2. MANAGEMENT

2.1 Organization

The tasks needed to create critical software for embedded systems project organization are designed to ensure clear lines of authority and to provide a framework within which administrative and technical control of software activities can be cost-effectively integrated into a quality product.

Primary responsibilities for various configuration management tasks are designed as shown in Table 1 {TBD}. Within project organization, the project manager has total responsibility for the project. The project manager serves as the project Configuration Control Board (CCB) chairperson. The SCM project authority from the SCM organization co-chairs the CCB.

The corporate Software Configuration Management authority may assist the project manager with tailoring of this Software Configuration Management Plan (SCMP) when the size and complexity of the project warrant a non-standard plan. In such a case, SCM-related procedures may also need to be tailored. The SCM authority has primary responsibility for everything concerning procedures and their adaptations.

The project manager, together with the SCM authority, have responsibility for overseeing implementation of the SCM Plan and procedures. The Software Configuration Management authority reports functionally to the corporate software manager for the implementation of this plan. Administratively, the SCM authority reports to the QA department, which performs the necessary activities for the project.

▶ **For prototype systems:**
There is probably no specific information change needed for this class of project.

▶ **For the maintenance project:**
In this project type, there may be a need for activities of specific subsections of the organization to be described. In such cases, it is recommended that this paragraph define these sub-organizations and their activities via separate subparagraphs.

▶ **For the product line systems:**
Unless there are specific business reasons for it, there is probably no specific information change needed for this class of project.

Checklist 13.1

- Has each and every aspect of the corporate's organization which deals with Configuration Management of software been described?
- Is this description accompanied with a graphic diagram?
- Have the Software Configuration Management related responsibilities of each part of the organization been specified, including interrelationships?
- Do these interrelationships include interfacing with the testing and QA organizations?
- Does the description of each organization include resources and personnel?

2.2 SCM responsibilities

2.2.1 Areas of SCM responsibilities

The Software Configuration Management authority has responsibility and authority to require changes in practices and procedures that do not meet contract requirements.

The general responsibilities of the Software Configuration Management authority are outlined below. The Software Configuration Management authority's functions include, but are not limited to, the following tasks:

1. Implementation and maintenance of the software configuration management plan
2. Configuration identification
3. Configuration control
4. Status accounting
5. Configuration Control Board co-chairperson
6. Establishment (with project manager) and maintenance of engineering baselines
7. Co-chairperson for formal audits
8. Participation in reviews and audits

The SCM authority's primary mission is to ensure visibility of all events during the product life-cycle.

2.2.2 Configuration item identification

Configuration identification is applied to all items related to software, both code and associated documentation. Associated documentation (that is, specifications, design documents, program/procedure listings, testing documentation, etc.) along with the actual produced software makes up the configuration item. The Software Configuration Management authority originates the identification scheme, with the approval of program management.

Configuration identification of computer programs and documentation during the development effort consists of established baselines and releases that are time dependent, according with development schedules, as described in the Software Development Plan.

2.2.3 Status accounting

A software system is used for tracking changes and generating reports. 'Changes files' — documenting deltas (time-dependent differences) between versions of configuration items — are maintained. Each project defines in its Software Development Plan:

(a) The status reports produced
(b) Their periodicity
(c) The recipients and distribution
(d) Security levels

2.2.4 Audits

The Software Configuration Management authority acts as co-chair of formal audits and chair of all informal (internal) audits.

A formal audit is performed as a part of the baseline process. All formal baselines and all user/field releases must be audited.

Each formal audit is preceded by an informal audit. The results of the informal audit are reported to project management. The results of the formal audit are reported to corporate management. At management's discretion, or at customer request, the formal audit report is passed to the customer for perusal and approval.

2.2.5 Configuration Control Board (CCB)

The CCB is established by the project manager and SCM authority.

The project manager is the CCB chairperson and has the final responsibility for CCB actions relative to project SCM policies, plans, procedures and interfaces. The Software Configuration Management authority acts as co-chair.

In addition to the two chairpersons, the CCB will always include a representative from software quality assurance and may include, on a temporary 'as-needed' basis:

(a) Development personnel
(b) Hardware representative
(c) Testing representative
(d) Customers

CCB meetings are held when required at the call of the CCB chairperson. The system/software change request that is generated is reviewed by the CCB and one of the following actions taken: approved, disapproved or frozen. In any case, the originator of the SCR is notified of the decision.

The changes needed to be made in Section 2.2, and all of its subparagraphs, should follow directly from the changes made in Section 2.1. If they do not, this probably means that Section 2.1 has not been clearly enough defined.

2.3   Interface control

Interface control is handled in the same manner as other types of hardware, software or documentation. Any differences between the SQAP and the SCMP must be resolved prior to the establishment of any baselines.

▶ **For prototype systems:**
Unless the project interfaces with another project or, even worse, another company, there is probably no specific information change needed for this class of project.

▶ **For the maintenance project:**
Is the hardware changing as well? What item's stability can be depended upon and which ones can clearly not be depended upon?

▶ **For the product line systems:**
The really important question here is almost always exactly *who* is responsible for the maintenance of *each and every* specific interface.

2.4 SCMP Implementation

2.4.1 Configuration Control Board

This function is project dependent. Each project manager is expected to define this function for the individual project. This definition must be added as a project-specific appendix to this document.

This section is part of Appendix 2 — SCM Management for the . . . Project.

2.4.2 Configuration baselines

This function is project dependent. Each project manager is expected to define this function for the individual project. This definition must be added as a project-specific appendix to this document.

This section is part of Appendix 2 — SCM Management for the . . . Project.

2.4.3 Schedules and procedures for SCM reviews and audits

This function is project dependent. Each project manager is expected to define this function for the individual project. This definition must be added as a project-specific appendix to this document.

This section is part of Appendix 2 — SCM Management for the . . . Project.

2.4.4 Configuration Management of software development tools

This function is project dependent. Each project manager is expected to define this function for the individual project. This definition must be added as a project-specific appendix to this document.

This section is part of Appendix 2 — SCM Management for the . . . Project.

▶ **For prototype systems:**
Section 2.4 *must* be greatly simplified for these projects.

▶ **For the maintenance project:**
Section 2.4 should probably be somewhat simplified for this project type. There may be a need for activities of specific subsections of the organization to be described, but this will be quite rare.

▶ **For the product line systems:**
The number one problem to be addressed is the release of new baseline to clients! This must be the central point of this paragraph.

2.5   Applicable policies, directives and procedures

This function is project dependent. Each project manager is expected to define this function for the individual project. This definition must be added as a project-specific appendix to this document.
This section is part of Appendix 2 — SCM Management for the . . . Project.

▶ **For prototype systems:**
There is probably no specific information change needed for this class of project.

▶ **For the maintenance project:**
Unless there are specific business reasons for not doing it, a very specific list is definitely in order. There may also be a need for specific directives to be described. In such cases, it is recommended that this paragraph define these via subparagraphs, as needed.

▶ **For the product line systems:**
Unless there are specific business reasons for not doing it, a very specific list is definitely in order.

3. SCM ACTIVITIES

3.1   Configuration identification

3.1.1 Documentation

This function is project dependent. Each project manager is expected to define this function for the individual project. This definition must be added as a project-specific appendix to this document.
This section is part of Appendix 3 — SCM Identification for the . . . Project.

3.1.2 Software parts

This function is project dependent. Each project manager is expected to define this function for the individual project. This definition must be added as a project-specific appendix to this document.
This section is part of Appendix 3 — SCM Identification for the . . . Project.

3.1.3 Configuration identification of the functional baseline

This function is project dependent. Each project manager is expected to define this function for the individual project. This definition must be added as a project-specific appendix to this document.
This section is part of Appendix 3 — SCM Identification for the . . . Project.

3.1.4 Configuration identification of the allocated baseline

This function is project dependent. Each project manager is expected to define this function for the individual project. This definition must be added as a project-specific appendix to this document.

This section is part of Appendix 3 — SCM Identification for the . . . Project.

3.1.5 Configuration identification of the developmental baseline

This function is project dependent. Each project manager is expected to define this function for the individual project. This definition must be added as a project-specific appendix to this document.

This section is part of Appendix 3 — SCM Identification for the . . . Project.

3.1.6 Configuration identification of the product baseline

This function is project dependent. Each project manager is expected to define this function for the individual project. This definition must be added as a project-specific appendix to this document.

This section is part of Appendix 3 — SCM Identification for the . . . Project.

▶ **For prototype systems:**
Identify project baselines and labelling techniques to be used for each and every item classification.

▶ **For the maintenance project:**
Remember to keep very tight control of the linkages between item types — for example a source code and its specifications, documentation, etc.

▶ **For the product line systems:**
Pay very close attention to naming conventions (sometimes called 'nomenclature') and questions of 'ownership' of all items.

3.2   Configuration control

Software Configuration Management and change control is applied to all documents, source and object code and all released items. Control is applied through implementation of configuration identification discipline, application of INTERSOLV Corporation's 'PVCS' — Version Manager and Configuration Builder software products, the Change Control Board (CCB) and status accounting functions.

All status accounting functions are processed via the Version Manager facilities.

3.2.1 Functions of the Configuration Control Board

The Configuration Control Board reviews proposed changes. The review includes:

(a) Assuring compliance with approved specifications and designs
(b) Evaluating impact on existing software
(c) Evaluating effects on operability of the product

(d) Evaluating effects on maintainability
(e) Estimating costs for both the analysis and implementation of the change

Each engineering change or problem report that is initiated against a formally identified configuration item is evaluated by the CCB to determine its necessity and impact.

The CCB members sign the document to indicate that they have reviewed the changes and provided their recommendations to the chairperson. The CCB approves, disapproves or freezes all changes. The mechanism for submitting changes to the software or documentation is the systems/software change request (see Appendix 5, Attachment B).

All CCB reviews and decisions are public. The originator of the change request is notified for follow-up.

3.2.2 The system/software change request

This form may be project dependent. Each project manager is expected to adapt a form for the individual project. This definition must be added as a project-specific appendix to this document.

This section is part of Appendix 3 — SCM Identification for the . . . Project.

Checklist 13.2

- Has a formal procedure been established defining the format of formal problem/change reports?
- Has a formal procedure been established defining the methodology of formal problem/change reports?
- Has a formal procedure been established defining the documentation of formal problem/change reports?
- Has a formal procedure been established defining the corrective action resulting from formal problem/change reports?
- Does the formal change/problem report include, at least, all of the following information:
  - system/project name
  - originator
  - problem number
  - problem name
  - software element(s) affected
  - document(s) affected
  - origination date
  - category and priority
  - description of problem
  - analyst
  - date assigned
  - date completed
  - analysis time
  - recommended solution
  - impacts

- problem status
- approval of solution
- follow-up action
- corrector
- correction date
- version number
- correction time
- implementation solution

3.2.3 Software change authorization

This form may be project dependent. Each project manager is expected to adapt a form for the individual project. This definition must be added as a project-specific appendix to this document.

This section is part of Appendix 3 — SCM Identification for the . . . Project.

3.2.4 Change control automated SCM tools

3.2.4.1 System libraries

The libraries of the system are used to control all textual files containing the specifications, documentation, test plans and procedures and source code. Each library is managed as a separate 'domain'. In each domain, there may exist as many physical libraries as the project domain coordinator (or project manager) deems necessary.

All of the libraries listed below are managed via the PVCS facilities on the local area network. Every day, at the beginning of work, at noon and at the end of the working day, the PVCS Production Gateway software is run to ensure synchronization of the LAN libraries with their equivalent libraries (when existent) upon the corporate mainframe.

The library structure that is used is as follows:

- The project master library
- The testing and integration library
- The development library

Each domain coordinator is responsible for a backup, once per day.

3.2.4.2 The project master library

The project master library contains all modules which have passed the relevant testing stages. For example: for code — integration tests; for requirements/design — SQA document audit.

3.2.4.3 The testing and integration library

The testing and integration library (T&I) contains modules which the developer has declared as 'finished' but are not yet fully tested. Modules are passed from the testing library to the project master library when all integration testing has been performed and no new information (such as error reports) can be discovered. Modules are passed back to the developer library whenever errors are discovered by the integration process.

3.2.4.4 The development library

The development library is a non-controlled area, under developer responsibility. Developers may utilize all software configuration control tools, at their discretion. Modules are passed to the testing library when the developer declares them 'finished'. When passed, the module is deleted from the developer's workspace.

▶ **For prototype systems:**
There is probably no specific information change needed for this class of project other than that, as this paragraph stands, it is definitely 'overkill' for this project type.

▶ **For the maintenance project:**
There is an absolute necessity to pay very strict attention to problem classifications and criteria used for prioritization of problem handling.

▶ **For the product line systems:**
There is an absolute necessity to pay very strict attention to problem classifications and criteria used for prioritization of problem handling. In this section, this classification (products) and the previous (maintenance) are essentially identical. In both cases, it is probably a very bad career move to mess up here.

Checklist 13.3

- Has a procedure been constructed for the management, implementation, development and control of the software development library/libraries?
- Does this procedure include all steps necessary for both the code and the documentation?
- Does this paragraph describe the contractor's procedures or provide a reference to the document which does?
- Have access procedures to the SDL been established and documented?

3.3 Configuration status accounting

This function is project dependent. Each project manager is expected to define this function for the individual project. This definition must be added as a project-specific appendix to this document.

This section is part of Appendix 3 — SCM Identification for the . . . Project.

▶ **For prototype systems:**
Keep this very simple. This is a minor function for this classification.

▶ **For the maintenance project:**
Define exactly which reports are to be issued for this project, to whom are they issued and at what frequency. Be prepared to defend what you write.

▶ **For the product line systems:**
Define exactly which reports are to be issued for this project, to whom they are issued and at what frequency. Be prepared to defend what you write.

3.4 Audits and reviews

3.4.1 Functional configuration audit

This function is project dependent. Each project manager is expected to define this function for the individual project. This definition must be added as a project-specific appendix to this document.

This section is part of Appendix 3 — SCM Identification for the . . . Project.

3.4.2 Physical configuration audit

This function is project dependent. Each project manager is expected to define this function for the individual project. This definition must be added as a project-specific appendix to this document.

This section is part of Appendix 3 — SCM Identification for the . . . Project.

3.4.3 Reviews

This function is project dependent. Each project manager is expected to define this function for the individual project. This definition must be added as a project-specific appendix to this document.

This section is part of Appendix 3 — SCM Identification for the . . . Project.

▶ **For prototype systems:**
It is very unlikely that there will be a need for project audits or reviews, other than a single acceptance review.

▶ **For the maintenance project:**
Is 'third-party software' a part of this project, this maintenance task? This is the most important set of items to be reviewed. For these items the review is critical.

▶ **For the product line systems:**
Every baseline must be thoroughly audited. These reviews must include development progress (all phases and steps) and all pre-release processes.

4 TOOLS, TECHNIQUES AND METHODOLOGIES

4.1 Configuration control tools

All Software Configuration Management activities use the computerized Software Configuration Management toolset marketed by the Intersolv Corporation, called PVCS. Though this toolset has many possible subsystems, only two of these products have been purchased at this time: PVCS Version Manager and PVCS Configuration Builder.

The PVCS Version Manager is used for all activities concerning the archiving of workfiles, of all file types. This includes all code files and all files that document, specify or define these files (e.g. files of presentation graphics — such as slides — written using a drawing program, word processing files containing product documentation or CASE files containing product definitions and specifications).

The PVCS Configuration Builder subsystem is used for all activities relating to compiling and linking of the modules from which the product is constructed. A footprint is used to retain information within the executable file. The author of Builder script files is usually the author of the program being built. However, the software configuration coordinator for the project (who is assumed to be the 'expert' for use of the PVCS Configuration Builder) has final responsibility for the content of any Builder script file. After the testing of these files, the build script is baselined and the project is provided with a compiled version. Any changes to these files must be authorized by the project manager and the changes made by both the product's developer and the SCM coordinator, in cooperation.

▶ **For prototype systems:**
Keep it very simple! Remember that for these types of projects speed is critical. There is frequently no need for anything more sophisticated than a manual card file.

▶ **For the maintenance project:**
In this project type, unless there are specific business reasons for it, there is probably no specific information change needed. That is, the same level of detail which appears above is needed.

▶ **For the product line systems:**
Unless there are specific business reasons for it, there is probably no specific information change needed for this class of project.

4.2   The techniques used for configuration control

This function is project dependent. Each project manager is expected to define this function for the individual project. This definition must be added as a project-specific appendix to this document.

This section is part of Appendix 4 — SCM Techniques for the . . . Project

▶ **For prototype systems:**
This section is probably unnecessary for this project type.

▶ **For the maintenance project:**
Pay a great deal of attention to specifics but this does not mean that one must go into a great amount of detail. The paragraph should be short, but specific.

▶ **For the product line systems:**
This section is probably unnecessary for this project type, unless there are specific business reasons for it.

4.3   The techniques used for Configuration Management

This function is project dependent. Each project manager is expected to define this function for the individual project. This definition must be added as a project-specific appendix to this document.

This section is part of Appendix 4 — SCM Techniques for the . . . Project.

▶ **For prototype systems:**
This section is probably unnecessary for this project type.

▶ **For the maintenance project:**
Pay a great deal of attention to specifics but this does not mean that one must go into a great amount of detail. The paragraph should be short, but specific.

▶ **For the product line systems:**
This section is probably unnecessary for this project type, unless there are specific business reasons for it.

4.4   Backup procedures

The backup function is a project-critical function. The development library must be backed up daily. The project master library must be backed up at least weekly. However, in addition to this, *this function is project dependent*. Each project manager is expected to define this function for the individual project. This definition must be added as a project-specific appendix to this document.

This section is part of Appendix 4 — SCM Techniques for the . . . Project.

▶ **For prototype systems:**
This section is probably unnecessary for this project type.

▶ **For the maintenance project:**
Critical, critical, critical! Mistakes in this area can be very bad career moves. Pay a great deal of attention to specifics. The paragraph may be short, but specific.

▶ **For the product line systems:**
This section is probably unnecessary for this project type, unless there are specific business reasons for it.

5 SUPPLIER CONTROL

The following section (including all subparagraphs) may be omitted from projects which do not have any vendor or supplier software items. Care should be taken as there are very rarely *no* products. The history of the profession has shown us that even very reliable vendors make mistakes. An example of this is the rash of 'viruses' reported to have been distributed by very large corporations, completely unintentionally, of course.

▶ **For prototype systems:**
This whole section is probably unnecessary for this project type.

5.1 Vendor-provided software

This function is project dependent. Each project manager is expected to define this function for the individual project. This definition must be added as a project-specific appendix to this document.

This section is part of Appendix 5 — SCM Supplier Control Techniques for the . . . Project.

▶ **For the maintenance project:**
Pay a great deal of attention to specifics. This does not mean that one must go into a great amount of detail. The paragraph should be short, but specific.

▶ **For the product line systems:**
This section is probably unnecessary for this project type, unless there are specific business reasons for it (e.g. do the third-party vendors have a continuing responsibility for the product's software?).

5.2 Subcontracted software

This function is project dependent. Each project manager is expected to define this function for the individual project. This definition must be added as a project-specific appendix to this document.

This section is part of Appendix 5 — SCM Supplier Control Techniques for the . . . Project.

▶ **For the maintenance project:**
Pay a great deal of attention to specifics but this does not mean that one must go into a great amount of detail. The paragraph should be short, but specific.

▶ **For the product line systems:**
This section is probably unnecessary for this project type, unless there are specific business reasons for it (e.g. do the third-party vendors have a continuing responsibility for the product's software?).

5.3 Vendor and subcontractor software

This function is project dependent. Each project manager is expected to define this function for the individual project. This definition must be added as a project-specific appendix to this document.

This section is part of Appendix 5 — SCM Supplier Control Techniques for the . . . Project.

▶ **For the maintenance project:**
Pay a great deal of attention to specifics but this does not mean that one must go into a great amount of detail. The paragraph should be short, but specific.

▶ **For the product line systems:**
This section is probably unnecessary for this project type, unless there are specific business reasons for it (e.g. do the third-party vendors have a continuing responsibility for the product's software?).

5.4 Security issues relating to vendor-supplied software items

This function relates to all software items supplied for the project — even if items of this type, from the same vendor, have been previously supplied. Beyond that, *this function is project dependent*. Each project manager is expected to define this function for the individual project. This definition must be added as a project-specific appendix to this document.

This section is part of Appendix 5 — SCM Supplier Control Techniques for the . . . Project.

▶ **For the maintenance project:**
Pay a great deal of attention to specifics but this does not mean that one must go into a great amount of detail. The paragraph should be short, but specific.

▶ **For the product line systems:**
This section is very necessary for this project type if a situation of third-party development still exists at this point.

Checklist 13.4

- Have all needed safeguards for the correct coordination of the contractor with project subcontractors been constructed?
- Can this coordination be clearly verified, as defined?

6 RECORDS COLLECTION AND RETENTION

This function is project dependent. Each project manager is expected to define this function for the individual project. This definition must be added as a project-specific appendix to this document.

This section is part of Appendix 6 — SCM Records Collection Techniques for the . . . Project.

▶ **For prototype systems:**
Copies of all status reports are retained for the duration of the project.

▶ **For the maintenance project:**
Pay attention to specifics. The paragraph should be quite short, but specific. A common retention period is five years.

▶ **For the product line systems:**
The backup databases of each release must be saved for the duration of the product's marketability. After the product is retired from the market some of them may be disposed of. However, even then, some of them (at least) must be retained for at least seven years. That is to say, the absolutely longest time one can possibly imagine the product to be still in use (plus a little bit more). *This is critical for litigation prevention/protection.*

APPENDIX — ISO 9000-3 MAPPING AND SUPPORT

Section 6 of ISO 9000, *Quality management and quality assurance standards; Part 3: Guidelines for the application of ISO 9001 to the development, supply and maintenance of software* — the guide to the application of the ISO 9001 standard for quality management to software — discusses supporting requirements for the quality system being implemented. Specifically, the requirements are those which are not *phase dependent*. This may mean (in most cases, it *should* mean) that they are applied to every phase of the development life-cycle.

Quite rightly, this section begins with *6.1 Configuration management*. Rightly, because Software Configuration Management is the most significant of all the non-phase oriented techniques that are discussed.

The basic mapping of the various clauses from each of the standards is summarized in Table 13.1. As one can see, it is rather confusing. Remember, *what you will be audited against is ISO 9001*, the centre column of the table.

Table 13.1 Clause comparison between the three documents

ISO 9000-3 clause	ISO 9001 clause	IEEE 828 clause
6.1.1	4.4, 4.5, 4.8	3.1.2, 3.1.3, 3.1.4, 3.1.5, 3.1.6, 3.2
6.1.2	4.12, 4.13	2
6.1.3.1	4.8	3.1.2, 3.1.3, 3.1.4, 3.1.5, 3.1.6
6.1.3.2	4.12, 4.13, 4.14	3.2
6.1.3.3	4.10.4	3.3
6.2	4.5	3.1.1, 3.2, 3.3

Clearly, any tool (or toolset) which one may choose must surpass the capabilities here demanded (*that* certainly should not be difficult).

Another interesting thing to be aware of is that, while ISO 9000-3 does not reference it, ISO 9004 can also be helpful — sometimes perhaps even more than ISO 9001. Particularly, one's attention should be drawn to Section 8, *Quality in specification and design*; Section 12, *Product verification*; and Section 15, *Corrective action*.

14

SOFTWARE LIFE-CYCLE

LIFE-CYCLE DEVELOPMENT CONCEPTS

This section briefly examines the concepts of managing a project via a modelling technique called 'life-cycle'. Clearly, this chapter does not pretend to fully describe this, very basic, concept of project management. The orientation of this discussion is towards the management of the software configurations. The life-cycle concept reflects both a 'phase-oriented' approach and a 'product-oriented' approach. The life-cycle model chosen here is specific to software development, from an internal point of view. Many other views are equally legitimate; for instance, the life-cycle model which one may choose for third-party software acquisition would certainly be quite different (see also, perhaps, IEEE Std-1062: *Recommended Practice for Software Acquisition*). There are also many others.

The following discussion examines both these concepts. The text describes the phase orientation. Figure 14.1 maps this to the product orientation. Phases are usually delineated by events, which are called milestones. An event is typically (though not always) characterized by the release of one or more specific software artifact(s). Frequently, a phase may be defined hierarchically, containing within it several 'subphases' or 'small' milestones. In any case, most of these will also be defined with the aid of some artifact. It is all of these software artifacts which must be 'zealously' stored (perhaps guarded) by the Software Configuration Management system.

THE PHASE-ORIENTED MODEL

We deal here with a simplified life-cycle model. That is to say, we deal with those phases of the life-cycle that are clearly agreed upon by all practitioners. If one is interested in delving into this in great detail, the IEEE Std-1074 probably gives the broadest coverage (a guideline to its use is being written and should be published by the end of 1994). Each of the commonly accepted phases of the software life-cycle must be used to provide pointers as to what the Software Configuration Management planner should be particularly aware of during each phase. The software configuration aspects of each of these phases is briefly examined.

	Allocated	Functional	High-level	Detailed	Testing	Operational
SDP	X					
SQAP		X				
SCMP		X				
System description	X					
S/W requirements spec.		X				
Database schema			X			
High-level design			X			
Module designs				X		
Module tree structure			X			
Module specifications				X		
Test plans		X				
Test designs			X			
Test procedures				X		
Test reports					X	
Load maps					X	
User manuals						X
Source code files					X	
Object code files					X	

Figure 14.1 Where materials need to be controlled.

DESIGN PHASE

We must remember that system and software functional requirements are becoming more complex — broader in scope and more demanding of levels of performance — with each passing year. System elements are becoming more distributed, with many tasks being performed across processors. And not just for embedded systems: even many transaction processing systems that previously appeared monolithic are now routinely split up as multiple communicating processes across many machines.

All design documents are tracked with the CM system from the moment they are agreed upon. The term 'design' is used in its broadest sense. These documents include all those relating to the requirements and the design of the system: system and software requirements; functional specifications; system and software design; interface specifications; high-level (top-level) design; low-level design (pseudo code); etc. All these documents have the same character from the configuration standpoint.

Do not attempt to manage design documents before they have been verified and agreed upon. This will almost always be counter-productive. In certain projects that this author is familiar with, the requirements/design documents began to be so complex, and the revision process so drawn out, that a decision had to be made to 'draw a line'.

This now creates a design baseline. It is very important to remember the expected lifetimes that systems survive. Many systems are expected to live for 14, 20 or 30 years. There will be an increasing need to modify these systems — because of changing requirements and new user expectations, changes in technology and corrections to compensate for hardware failures. All this obliges frequent reuse of materials.

From this baseline the project can now proceed in a much more coherent and consistent manner.

IMPLEMENTATION PHASE

All code generation should be performed together with the actions of a Configuration Management system. The project should not wait until the project is in maintenance. Every initial and intermediate revision should be archived.

One very useful way of doing this is via predefined control areas. We call these control areas 'universes' or domains. Such predefined areas may include a developer's universe, a tester's universe and a release universe. Each one of these domains can (and probably should) be managed separately. This maximizes independence of the various domains and efficient resource usage with system security. The SCM system is used to enhance all aspects of the system's management. This differentiation between the universes is also used to 'sift' unneeded revisions, created by (for instance) the development process — there is no need to store them for corporate posterity.

TESTING PHASE

The concept of 'system integration' is the building of the parts being joined together to form a whole system (this is frequently called a 'build'). This can also be used to describe the incremental construction of a prototype (a working model) and gradually building it up into a full system. Many times these two strategies (builds or prototypes) can be combined for a very efficient method of system build. In any case, during the course of constructing a system, several versions will usually exist.

During this phase, documentation is likely to be finalized and stored (archived). The types of documentation to be expected during this phase include user documentation, technical maintenance documentation and training. The archival system must be utilized both for the building/integration process and for the documentation.

The extended life of systems obliges frequent reuse of materials. Clearly, one classification of materials which are extensively reused is the test materials! They must be placed under very strict Configuration Management. Also, persistent links must be established between sets of test materials and system versions throughout the life-cycle. This should probably be a part of the System/Software Quality Plan or the System Verification and Validation Plan — in parallel to the SCM Plan.

The plan must define all procedures (and, of course, tools) used for the CM of the test materials. Test materials are defined to include, at least: test plans, test procedures, test scripts, test data, expected results, actual results and any test reports and analyses. As usual, all aspects of the SCM (identification, control, etc.) must be managed. However, the naming conventions must take into account the special characteristics caused by the intimacy of the relationship that this material has with the applicable system products.

BETA TEST PHASE

This phase is characterized by a high degree of interaction of developers with a small, select group of users. These users generate bug reports, which in turn force bug fixes to be produced. All this must be done within a very short time frame. The bugs may have many different characteristics. They may reflect both internal and/or external errors. These errors may be logic, design, documentation and/or code errors. This is where the SCM system really gets its workout! If the system is powerful and properly organized, at this point comes the really big payoff. If the wrong tools have been chosen, this is where the big price is going to be paid.

RELEASE PHASE

When the final release is ready, the organization must be prepared to handle code and finalized documentation, and everything must completely match! Quality assurance activities must be finalized. And, of course, shipments must begin. All this must be done correctly. Configuration Management errors are one of the most common types of error in this stage. Historically, we know that care is simply not sufficient.

MAINTENANCE PHASE

The maintenance phase of a project is characterized by standard maintenance tasks, including system enhancements, intermingled with problem reports and emergency bug fixes. Once again, these problems may indicate either internal and/or external errors. These errors may be logic, design and/or code errors or they may be indicative of documentation problems. The SCM system is a vital resource for controlling the process of change that all this entails. Remember, probably more than 80 per cent of the total cost of the system is spent during this phase. This phase is actually a very large set of all the other phases, repeated *ad nauseam* (sometimes it appears to be *ad infinitum* but, fortunately, this is an illusion).

DOCUMENT STORAGE, HANDLING AND RELEASE

In parallel with this phase-oriented life-cycle model, one must also pay very close attention to issues involving the various deliverables or materials which the project must deliver. That is, any life-cycle model used for Software Configuration Management must be both phase oriented and product oriented. See Fig. 14.1 for a mapping of the various materials to the baselines where they begin to be controlled. Also, see Checklist 14.1 for the completion of this concept.

Checklist 14.1

- Have all deliverable and non-deliverable items which are to be developed as part of the project been identified and clearly labelled?
- Have all deliverable and non-deliverable items which are to be purchased as part of the project been identified and clearly labelled?
- Does the project include client-supplied items which will need to be stored?
- Does the project include client-supplied items which will need to be included within another object (item) which will need to be stored?
- Have the storage and handling requirements been identified?
- Are all documents which are significant to the success of the project formally controlled?
- Are all documents stored in the official corporate or project Configuration Management system?
- Does the software for the computerized Configuration Management system use a known tool, with a significant market share?
- Have all changes to controlled documents been processed through proper channels, using the appropriate engineering change notices and/or change request forms?
- Are backup and master copies of each controlled document stored off-site?
- Can they be accessed within 24 hours in the event of catastrophe?
- Is the document creation process auditable for document security, integrity and efficiency?
- Does the Configuration Management system allow traceability of changes to the documents from previous releases?
- Does the Configuration Management system allow on-call back-tracking of the documents to previous releases?
- Are release procedures documented via a Software Configuration Management Plan?
- Are all project media created via an efficient and auditable system?
- Are all removable project media (e.g. tapes, diskettes, etc.) formally controlled?
- Have all changes to media been processed through proper channels, using the appropriate engineering change notices and/or change request forms?
- Are backup and master copies of all controlled media stored off-site?
- Can they be accessed within 24 hours in the event of catastrophe?

15

ORGANIZATION OF THE PROJECT IN THE LIGHT OF SCM

This chapter is really a set of 'tips' on methods of organization. You may like to use one of these sample structures for computer systems being utilized for development of your product. There are probably three possible 'configurations' for your project. Certainly, there may be quite legitimate variations on them. These methods are presented as 'prototypical' methods from which you may adopt that method most suitable for your project. Each of the following sections deals with one of these three major configurations.

SINGLE-PERSON, MULTI-PROJECT

In many organizations each developer works essentially alone, with little or no interaction between peers. This condition may be the result of devotion of a majority of the programmer's time to maintenance (the programmer is maintaining an existing application) rather than new development work. This, of course, is quite legitimate, providing it is not brought to ridiculous extremes.

As an example of a 'ridiculous extreme': in a certain bank that this author has consulted for, there are programmers engaged in maintenance of a specific application for periods of even 10 years. (This is not stifling of creativity: this is absolute assurance that you have killed it.)

In reasonable cases, this may be a very good method of organization. A very positive case with which this author is familiar is a company that has some 70 software developers working on products in the area of data communications. Each product is fairly small. There is a very large overlap of modules and professional knowledge between products. The average project length is about three months. The Software Configuration Management function became noticeably needed when they had a few hundred products released, with some 20 or 30 new releases a year.

Suddenly, the quality assurance function and the product testing function realized that they had lost control of the development process:

1. They were spending large amounts of time redoing software that had been developed once and could have been reused.
2. Tools, and their versions, were getting confused.
3. Tests were getting lost and could not be reused effectively (plans, designs and test cases).
4. Management had no method of controlling the projects or of measuring efforts being invested.
5. The documentation of these systems had become hopeless.

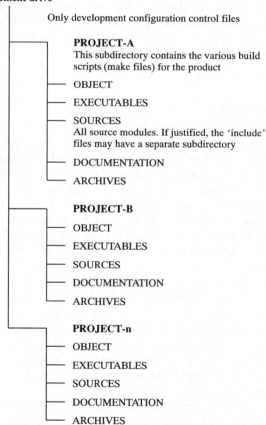

Development drive

Only development configuration control files

PROJECT-A
This subdirectory contains the various build scripts (make files) for the product

— OBJECT

— EXECUTABLES

— SOURCES
All source modules. If justified, the 'include' files may have a separate subdirectory

— DOCUMENTATION

— ARCHIVES

PROJECT-B
— OBJECT

— EXECUTABLES

— SOURCES

— DOCUMENTATION

— ARCHIVES

PROJECT-n
— OBJECT

— EXECUTABLES

— SOURCES

— DOCUMENTATION

— ARCHIVES

Figure 15.1   Directory suggestion for single-person, multi-project.

Clearly, a Software Configuration Management system was needed. Luckily, a network had already been implemented for effective use of other development tools, so that the only cash investment which needed to be made was the CM software itself. Of course, there was a need for discipline as well: both developer and management discipline.

The recommended organization is to create a separate logical (or physical) disk for development. This may be simply a directory tree or something more 'hard'. Under this directory structure, create a directory for each development or maintenance project. Each project directory will be a tree containing all of the files of that project, in subdirectories which group files by function. One of these subdirectories will be for the archive files (see Fig. 15.1). In this organization, a configuration administrator is unnecessary.

It should also be noted that there are two variants on this concept, which one may call 'small' or 'large' projects (even though they are single-person projects). A small project consists of one which involves only a very limited amount of files, say under about 25. In this kind of situation, even the simple organization displayed by Fig. 15.1 is not really needed. Perhaps even everything (source, object, documentation, build scripts, archives) can be done within one directory.

In the larger kind of task, involving more than about 25 files, we strongly recommend usage of a discipline similar to that described above. To ensure control, the level of clutter must be controlled. It is important to limit the quantity of files in each directory. Certainly, revision locking is the most critical SCM function here.

MULTI-PERSON, SINGLE-PROJECT

Many development projects occupy a whole organization. That is to say, the entire organization is organized for this development or perhaps even created for this project.

This situation demands a great deal of coordination and synchronization between the developers, between the developers and management, and with all other interested parties (e.g. QA/SQA, CM/SCM, administration functions, client communication, etc.). This implies that a powerful facility for access control must be used to protect files from unauthorized changes. Also, a LOGIN facility should be used for control of identification of whatever user is accessing the files. This discussion assumes the use of a local area network. Most LANs have this facility.

The first task will be to create a directory tree structure on the network for the project's files. This structure must include a separate subdirectory for each type of file. This directory structure, less the archive subdirectory, should be duplicated on each developer's local disk drive. Be careful to ensure that the configuration file and the access database be made read-only and not accessible by anyone on the project other than the person authorized as the configuration administrator. There should be only one single configuration control file (a single access control database should be obvious at this point) to ensure that everyone uses the same settings (see Fig. 15.2).

The implementation of a journalizing feature is essential for this type of project. Other functions which are highly recommended (but, unfortunately, not supported by many SCM systems) are semaphores, multiple-revision-locking and life-cycle management. (These functions can be dispensed with if the system being developed is less than, say, 20 staff-years or particularly simple.)

Semaphores are a computer facility ensuring exclusive access to shared archives. This coordinates the actions of individual developers and ensures that clashes do not occur — exceedingly important!

Network drive

- **PROJECT**
  This subdirectory contains the various build
  scripts (make files) for the product and
  development configuration control files

- EXECUTABLES

- OBJECT

- SOURCES
  All source modules. If justified, the 'include'
  files may have a separate subdirectory

- DOCUMENTATION

- ARCHIVES

Figure 15.2   Directory suggestion for multi-person, single-project.

Multiple-revision-locking permits a user to lock more than one revision in an archive file or to place more than one lock per revision. This allows the kind of complex processing which is necessary when major systems are being developed.

Life-cycle management allows the developer or project management to define and track the progress of a particular module (or set of modules) throughout the development cycle. That is, a module can be declared to be at the phase of (say) beta testing. A report can be produced to display which modules are at each phase of development and what is their rate of progress. Increased dimensions of access control can be implemented via this facility. This allows a great deal of control and visibility over the whole project.

Another good idea is to create all the archive files (as empty files) before they are used. After they are created, do not allow developers to create archive files on their own. The SCM system should have a facility to implement this. This prevents a large amount of 'silly' mistakes from occurring. These kinds of mistakes may cost the project a large effort, unnecessarily.

Remember that the backup function is a project-critical function which must be centrally controlled.

An interesting variant on this kind of project is a multi-person project which is developed without a network. (The above text assumes a network linkage between the developers.) This is certainly the most difficult type of project organization! The most common SCM solution is to assign one computer as the central repository — the central software configuration management database. The organization of this computer should be based upon that of the larger single-person project above. The check-out/check-in procedures must be performed either via one individual (a sort of project librarian) or performed by each team member accessing the 'central' PC and transferring the files via a diskette. A librarian will be needed for the larger projects, say more than three developers.

Remember, a primary danger here is to lose control of who has performed the change (the developer must identify him or herself to the system before each access). The most effective way to handle this is to demand that each developer bring a personalized configuration file on the transfer diskette. The SCM system should be used to enforce this discipline.

MULTI-PERSON, MULTI-PROJECT

This situation also demands the same kind of coordination and synchronization between parties involved as the previous example, except that here it is more complex. This coordination must certainly be between the developers, between the developers and management, and with all other interested parties (e.g. QA/SQA, CM/SCM, administration functions, client communication, etc.).

However, this same type of 'communication' must also be prevented between those that have no need to communicate. This is not 'Big Brother'. This is prudent management of the difficult and complex task of software development. It is as prudent and important as the use of passwords. Please do not fool yourselves into thinking that this is unimportant. Myriad errors can, and do, occur with improper organization.

Incidentally, multi-project may sometimes mean simply a very large single project, logically broken up for easier management.

This demands that powerful facilities for access control be used to protect files from unauthorized changes. A LOGIN facility is essential for control and identification of users accessing the files. This discussion assumes the use of a local area network. Most LANs have at least part of this facility.

The first task will be to create a separate directory tree structure on the network for each project's files. This structure includes subdirectories for each type of file. These directory structures, less the archive subdirectory, must be duplicated on the local drive of each developer involved for each project. Remember that users will retain only those source files that they are currently working on. Figure 15.3 illustrates this.

Care must be taken to ensure that the master configuration file and access database is read-only and not accessible by anyone on any project. They must be accessible by the person authorized as the configuration administrator only. There should be only one single configuration control file (a single access control database should be obvious at this point) to ensure that everyone uses the same settings.

Large projects must be partitioned into separate 'subtrees' for each project function. Each subtree should contain separate directories for sources, objects, documents, archives, scripts, etc.

Remember that the backup function is a critical management function which must be centrally controlled for all projects. This cannot, and must not, be left to chance.

The implementation of a journalizing feature is mandatory for this organization. Other functions which must be implemented and used are semaphores, multiple-revision-locking, life-cycle management and archive file creation control. (These functions can be dispensed with if the system being developed is less than, say, 20 staff-years or particularly simple.) Also, compression of archive files may be necessary.

Semaphores are a computer facility ensuring exclusive access to shared archives. This coordinates the actions of individual developers and ensures that clashes do not occur — exceedingly important!

Multiple-revision-locking permits users to lock more than one revision in an archive file or to place more than one lock per revision. This implements complex processing necessary for major systems development.

Life-cycle management allows developers and project management to define and track progress of sets of modules throughout the development and maintenance life-cycle. A module may be declared to be at the phase of (say) beta testing. A report can be produced

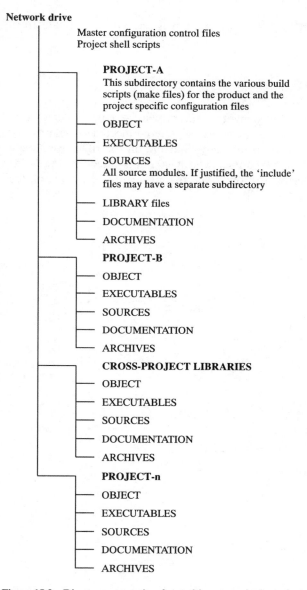

Figure 15.3 Directory suggestion for multi-person, single-project.

to display which modules are at each phase of development and what is their rate of progress. Increased dimensions of access control can be implemented via this facility. This allows a great deal of control and visibility over the whole project.

Create all archive files as empty files before use. After their creation, do not allow developers to create archive files on their own. The SCM system chosen must have a facility to implement this. The access privileges implemented must be composite functions defining several levels of access and control. These privileges must be defined to persons or groups only as needed. Make certain that this information is encrypted and safe from prying eyes.

MANAGEMENT BY 'DOMAINS'

Finally, a word about the conceptual management of the project. A convenient way to think about a project's organization is as a series of interconnected 'domains' or 'universes'. Figure 15.4 depicts this concept graphically. Starting on the right, we have a domain of the actual product. This is, of course, wholly administrated by the SCM system. Changes to this may be performed only via management's duly appointed representative — quality assurance or the CCB.

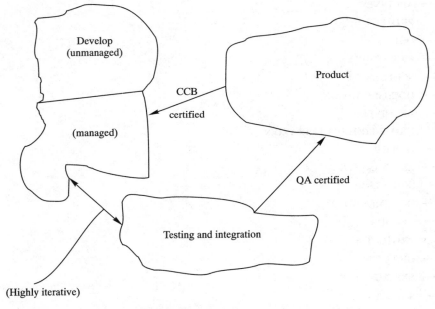

Figure 15.4   A conceptual project development environment.

On the left is the domain of software development. This domain is partially managed (via the SCM system) and partially open. The proportion must be decided on an ad hoc basis by the developers and their direct managers.

The final domain is that of integration and test. This will usually be administrated by the SCM system, for convenience (it should be considered whether this is needed).

The arrows show the direction of data flow (data in this sense consists of programs). There is only one bi-directional flow, and it is highly iterative. Everything else must be very strictly unidirectional.

16

THE RELATIONSHIP WITH HARDWARE CONFIGURATION MANAGEMENT

MULTI-DISCIPLINARY CROSS-FERTILIZATION

As was stated in the Introduction, Software Configuration Management is one of the areas in which the software community has learned from the hardware engineering community. This brief chapter is not intended to teach hardware engineers about Configuration Management. The objective is to teach software engineers how their partners in the development process are thinking when Configuration Management is discussed. This is accomplished by a comparison between the two disciplines and describing a general outline of a typical HCM system. This assumes that the reader is familiar with what has already been discussed in this book and that the system discussed is a computerized system.

There are a few basic differences between Hardware Configuration Management and Software Configuration Management. A very important point to begin with is that the Software Configuration Management system/discipline is 'physically' controlling the actual data items (configuration items) — as much as software can be called physical. It is simultaneously controlling and coordinating many different configurations and representations of the software (specifications, designs, source and executable code and test items). A Hardware Configuration Management system manages only documentation and information about the configuration items, as opposed to the items themselves. This is the most critical difference.

Software development environments are rapidly automating and converting into interactive and integrated toolsets. This is changing many of the 'traditional' methods and tools used for development of software. The integration of the Software Configuration Management system into the total development environment has caused a departure from the inherent simplicity of Hardware Configuration Management, without a departure from the fundamental concepts of CM. It is relevant to note that there is a quite fundamental shift in Hardware CM as a result of the increased integration of software into its process, as well.

Basically, there are five types of information which must be managed by the HCM system:

1. Configuration items and their bills-of-materials
2. Engineering change proposals and notices
3. Technical documents
4. Contracts
5. Action items

The following sections detail each of these information types.

CONFIGURATION ITEMS AND THEIR BILLS-OF-MATERIALS

Most configuration items are aggregates of hardware and/or software items. Many of these items may, in turn, be aggregates. This hierarchy descends until the smallest discrete portion/item is reached.

One would usually expect that the information managed for this item would consist of some combination of the following data items (this list is not meant to be exhaustive).

Firstly, of course, the basic identification information is needed. That probably means a serial number and a brief textual description of the item. In addition, it is important to know who the manufacturer of the item is and all organizational responsibilities. These responsibilities include both those of the manufacturer and of the user of the equipment.

Certainly, the history of the part is significant. This will consist of the milestones through which it has gone and all of the various technical reviews. Another very important item of information is the part's effectiveness. That is, how current is the part, and what are its various uses.

Finally, all of the documentation which refers to this item must be 'pointed to'. This includes, of course, all technical documentation and managerial documentation, such as contracts which refer to the item. It is important to understand this concept of 'pointed to'. Remember, the hardware is not directly managed. Therefore, the usual hardware engineer is not directly aware of the ability of a Software Configuration Management system to manage the documentation — which is, of course, produced today on-line. This is not any sort of criticism of the hardware engineers. But, certainly, this is one area where we software people can pay them back some of our 'debt' for what we learned from them.

ENGINEERING CHANGE PROPOSALS AND NOTICES

The engineering change proposal is the equivalent, for the hardware world, of the forms that have been described in this book for controlling the process of change. It is important to remember that hardware changes both more slowly and much less frequently than software. The major objective of this system is to provide a method of traceability of the part, particularly historically. One needs to control and maintain two main kinds of information: what is the exact status of the part and how did we get there.

This aspect of the system needs to also handle all information concerning deviations and waivers, in addition to the change proposals and notices. Once again, all documentation must be referenced and pointed to.

TECHNICAL DOCUMENTS

The two previous sectors referred to the concept of 'pointing to' documentation. This part of the HCM system is where the actual information concerning this documentation is stored. As a matter of fact, this concept is missing from most Software Configuration Management systems. For a modern SCM system to implement this should not be very difficult, as all of the information is already there (on the computer).

All parts specifications must be listed. Together with these specifications, their associated drawings and parts lists must also be managed. And, of course, the third 'leg' of any technical documentation, all the testing documentation, must also be accessible here. It may frequently be very important to also maintain a listing of any standards which are applicable to each of these documents. Finally, the revision information of all these documents must be maintained.

CONTRACTS

This idea is very similar to that of the technical documentation. The difference, of course, is that this classification does not refer to technical matters but to the managerial documents. The prototypical managerial document is the contract. Occasionally, for large projects, there may be only one contract which is relevant. However, in many organizations there may be a rather long list of contracts.

The actual contract is not the only item of information. What is needed is the contractual information. This includes prices, deliveries and venues. Many of these items may need to have their history maintained and accessible.

ACTION ITEMS

This final information classification is an interesting one. An action item is any sort of comment which must be acted upon. The comment may have been received from an audit or a review, but may also come up naturally during the course of a technical meeting or a meeting with the prospective user of the system. Action items do not necessarily deal only with changes, and certainly, not only with problems or anomalies — though these are the most common result of them.

Once again, this is fairly common practice for hardware engineers but still not typical for software. When the projects are large this may prove to be most helpful.

The data entity representing the action items must consist of the usual identification and reference information, as well as descriptions of the originator and those responsible. However, in addition to all this, one would expect to manage all of the dates and status information. Of course, beyond all this, one must also store the information which is the actual action item — i.e. the text of the actual comment or complaint that needs to be acted upon.

SUMMARY

This brief chapter teaches neither hardware engineers nor software engineers about Hardware Configuration Management. The objective is to show the readers of this book, the software engineering community, how partners in the development process are thinking when Configuration Management is discussed. This is particularly significant when the project is complex and includes both hardware and software development.

The chapter describes a general outline of a typical Hardware Configuration Management system. We have assumed that the reader is familiar with the major information already discussed in the book. It is to be hoped that this additional information will prove useful for improving the level of communication within major projects.

Appendix 1

EXERCISE 1 CONSTRUCTING THE CONFIGURATION MANAGEMENT PLAN

This exercise is based upon a concept of a 'workshop forum' of no more then 20 people. For the purposes of this exercise, the workshop forum should be divided into groups of two to three people. Care must be taken that the whole forum has the identical concept of the needs to be addressed by the Software Configuration Management Plan. Each group is assigned to write a specific section of the Plan.

The Plan will be written according to the IEEE 828 Standard as it appears in Chapter 13 of this book. The assignments will concern the following topics:

Environment

- Hardware of the system
- Hardware to be used for the CM system
- Operating systems
- Databases used
- Languages used
- Additional programming tools applied to the project which the CM system needs to account for

Management

- Of the project — concerning CM
- Of the product
- Of the Software Configuration Management system
- Of the process of SCM report distribution

Product assurance

- Describe how the CM is intended to aid in assuring the defined level of quality of the product(s) being produced
- Describe how the CM system will be used to enhance the client's 'Level of Confidence'

Usability

- Of the CM system (user friendliness, reporting procedures, etc.)

Standards

- Standards affected by CM
- Standards affecting CM

User viewability

- Of what?
- Access controls

In terms of the exercise, the major criterion for judging the success of the exercise will be that the plan can all fit together as a coherent document, even though it was written by disjoint groups.

There is, of course, no one 'correct' answer to this exercise, nor should there be. The quality of the exercise should be checked against Chapter 13.

EXERCISE 2   AN EXERCISE IN PLANNING SCM CONTENT

This exercise is also based upon workshop forums, with the same format as the previous exercise. The workshop forum should be divided into groups of two to three people, with a minimum of six working groups. Care must be taken that the whole forum has begun from identical concepts of SCM needs to be addressed.

This must be a practical exercise. The objective of the exercise is to provide the student with experience in tailoring the SCM activities described by this book to a specific organization or project.

1. Each participant group is to define a software development product to be developed as a project. The projected project size will approximate ten staff-years. Define all project stages and deliverables.

   The definitions are then exchanged between groups. (This exercise uses this technique several times. We suggest using some sort of technique of 'revolving' the definitions so that they are not simply exchanged between two partner groups.)
2. The second step is to define the software organization which is to develop the product. Remember to keep the organization *real*, not theoretical! We suggest that care be taken in the definition of the CCB — keep it practical and workable. Rotate the definitions to new groups.

3. Define the SCM methodologies, techniques and tools to be used for this development. If these tools and techniques have deliverables, briefly define them and to whom they apply. The practices defined must account for all development phases. Emphasize control and future maintenance needs (if this project has them: they do not always exist).

   Rotate the definitions to new groups.
4. Define, in detail, the process of software status accounting for the project. Make certain that all information needs are addressed and that, conversely, the recipients of all information-sets (reports) are really going to want them.

   Rotate the definitions to new groups.
5. The final stage is to attempt to simulate the action of the project, in the light of the SCM definitions. The groups should now define where each project is in the life-cycle.

   Introduce a problem into the process (e.g. a significant requirements change or a major rewrite of some of the software). As per the SCM process which has been defined, what now happens to the project?

   Rotate the definitions to new groups.

There is, of course, no one 'correct' answer to this exercise, nor should there be.

EXERCISE 3   DEFINE A SCM AUDIT

This exercise is based upon individual work. This must be a very practical exercise. The objective of the exercise is to provide the student with experience in creating a realistic checklist to be used for auditing SCM activities, as described by this book, and apply it to a specific organization or project.

As usual, there is no one 'correct' answer to this exercise, nor should there be. The objective is for the student to create an applicable checklist for a particular aspect of SCM activities.

The instructor should define to the students what their specific assignments are. Each student should receive a narrow range of applicability for which the checklist is to be constructed.

Appendix 2

ADDITIONAL READING

After having read this book, the reader may be interested in delving deeper into the subject of Software Configuration Management. While there is no shortage of material in the literature, there is certainly much less than one might expect to find on such a critical subject. For instance, a survey of several recent volumes of *Proceedings from the American Society of Quality Control* (1987, 1989 and 1990) shows a complete lack of information!

Generally speaking, most of the published literature contains information which has been designed for a specific need or application (such as large military-like projects or another specific application area) or to demonstrate a specific idea.

Frequently, after one has the background to be able to manage the information presented, even much of this specific information may prove to be very helpful.

The following lists are divided into three sections: books, articles and reports. Probably, most of the reports will not be generally available. The books and articles certainly are.

In any case, these lists are certainly not exhaustive — they are meant to be representative. Generally much of the 'chaff' has been eliminated. Those items which this author's experience has shown to be somewhat useful have been included. Other items which the reader may find useful, though somewhat less so, have also been included to strengthen the list.

This section does not include standards — see Appendix 3.

BOOKS

Babich, Wayne A. (1986) *'Software Configuration Management' Coordination for Team Productivity* Addison-Wesley, Wokingham, UK.

Bell System Technical Journal (1978) 'The UNIX time-sharing System', ISSN0005-8580, **57**, 6.

Bersoff, Edward H., Henderson, Vilas D. and Siegel, Stanley G. (1980) *Software Configuration Management. An Investment in Product Integrity* , Prentice-Hall, Englewood Cliffs, NJ.

Berlack, Ronald (1991) *Software Configuration Management*, Lockheed-Sanders Associates.

Buckle, J. K. (1982) *Software Configuration Management*, Macmillan, Basingstoke.

Cave, William C. and Maymon, Gilbert W. (1984) *Software Lifecycle Management, The Incremental Method*, The Macmillan DataBase/Data Communications Series, Macmillan, Basingstoke.

DeMillo, Richard A., McCracken, W. Michael, Martin, R. J. and Passafiume, John F. (1987) *Software Testing and Evaluation*, The Benjamin/Cummings Publishing Company, Inc.

Deutsch, Michael S. (1982) *Software Verification and Validation — Realistic Project Approaches*, Prentice-Hall Series in Software Engineering, Prentice-Hall, Englewood Cliffs, NJ.

Evans, Michael W. (1984) *Productive Software Test Management*, Wiley–Interscience Publication, John Wiley & Sons, Chichester.

Ferraby, Lyn (1991) *Change Control During Computer Systems Development*, Prentice-Hall, Englewood Cliffs, NJ.

Hed, Sven R., *Project Control Manual*, Sven R. Hed.

Martin, James and McClure, Carma (1983) *Software Maintenance: The Problem and its Solutions*, Prentice-Hall, Englewood Cliffs, NJ.

Raheja, Dev G. (1991) *Assurance Technologies, Principles and Practices*, McGraw-Hill Engineering and Technology Management Series, McGraw-Hill, New York, USA.

Whitgift, David (1991) *Methods and Tools for Software Configuration Management*. Logica Cambridge Ltd.

The PATRIARCH Software Quality Assurance Handbook, MIV~Meda Ltd, Catalog Number 2000.

The PATRIARCH Configuration Management Manual, MIV~Meda Ltd, Catalog Number 2140.

The PATRIARCH Management Procedures Manual, MIV~Meda Ltd, Catalog Number 3200.

ARTICLES

Bazelmans, Rudy (1985) 'Evolution of Configuration Management', *ACM SIGSOFT Software Engineering Notes*, **10**, 5.

Bersoff, Edward H., Henderson, Vilas D.and Siegel, Stan (1979) *Software Configuration Management*, Problem Management Series, Project Scheduling and Control, Auerbach Publishers Inc., USA.

Bersoff, Edward H. (1984) 'Elements of Software Configuration Management', *IEEE Transactions on Software Engineering*, **SE-10**, 1.

Blum, Joseph (1984) 'Computerized Software Configuration Management System, an ORACLE Relational DBMS Implementation', *Israel Software Quality Assurance Conference*, October 1984.

Buckle, J. K. (1983) 'Software Configuration Management: an Approach to Project Organization' (source unknown).

Collins, Frank (1983) *Change Management Strategies*, Systems Management Series, Auerbach Publishers Inc., USA.

Cottam, Ian D. (1984) 'The Rigorous Development of a System Version Control Program', *IEEE Transactions on Software Engineering*, **SE-10**, 2.

Davis, Alan M. (1985) 'Customized Automated Configuration Management', *Joint STARS Business Practices Workshop*, US Department of Defense.

Gibson, Cyrus F. and Davenport, Thomas H. (1985) 'Systems Change: Managing Organizational and Behavioral Impact', *Information Strategy: The Executive's Journal*, Fall.

Katz, Randy H. and Lehman, Tobin J. (1984) 'Database Support for Versions and Alternatives of Large Design Files', *IEEE Transactions on Software Engineering*, **SE-10**, 2.

Kinnaird, Richard (1987) 'Configuration Management for Software Engineering', *EXE Magazine,* June.

McCarthy, Rita (1975) 'Applying the technique of Configuration Management to Software', *Quality Progress*.

REPORTS

Problem and Change Control at the State of Washington Data Processing Service Center, Report Number GK20-1073-0, Installation Management series, IBM, undated.

Change Man Takes on a Challenging Endeavor, Report Number P-420-540, Software Engineering Strategies, Gartner Group, Inc., 5 April 1991.

Change Management Workbook, Report Number G320-8013-0, IBM, May 1982.

Problem and Change Management in Data Processing, A Survey and Guide, Report Number GE19-5201-0, IBM, August 1976.

Bryan, William and Siegel, Stan (1984) *Software Configuration Management (SCM)*, Grumman-CTEC Publication No. 84-ISD-034, Grumman-CTEC, Inc., Course Workbook.

Butler, Robert A. (1985) *Integrated Logistics Support, Implementation and Management*, Technology Training Corporation, Course Workbook.

Cherkovsky, D. (1988) *Software Change Control Procedure*, Report Number B-D110.0010.01.20-4.01, Israel Aircraft Industries Ltd, TAMAM.

Cherkovsky, D. (1988) *Software Problem Reporting and Corrective Action Procedure*, Report Number B-D110.0010.02.20-4.00, Israel Aircraft Industries Ltd, TAMAM.

Dean, J. W. (1983) *Advanced Configuration Management*, Technology Training Corporation, Course Workbook.

Dean, J. W. (1986) *Advanced Configuration Management II*, Technology Training Corporation, Course Workbook.

Reifer, Donald J. and Reifer Consultants, Inc., *Israel Aircraft Industries, Hardware/ Software Configuration Management, Training Seminar*, Course Workbook.

Reifer, Donald J., Knudson, Richard W. and Smith, Jerry (1987) *Final Report: Software Quality Survey*, American Society for Quality Control (ASQC), 20 November.

Thompson, K. and Ritchie, D. M. (1975) *UNIX Programmer's Manual, Sixth Edition*, Bell Telephone Laboratories, Inc.

Ziegler, Kurt Jr. (1978) *Improving Stability in Large Systems (A Management System)*, DAPS Code 0933, GG22-9051-00, IBM.

Appendix 3

STANDARDS

MILITARY

United States Department of Defense standards are used by all NATO countries and many other states which extensively use military equipment manufactured by the United States.

Other countries may also have military standards relating to the subject but they are used almost exclusively by their developers. As such, they are 'in-house' standards and not commonly known outside. There did not seem to be any reason to provide details here.

This is a much abbreviated list. The full list of United States Department of Defense Standards relating to Software and/or Configuration Management is several pages long. All the following documents are published by the United States Government, Department of Defense.

1. DoD-Std-2167A 'Military Standard; Defense System Software Development', 1988. (Supersedes DoD-Std 2167.) DoD-Std 2167; 'Defense system software development', Military standard; 1985.
2. DoD-Std-2168 'Military Standard; Defense System Software Quality Program'.
3. DoD-Std-480 'Configuration Control, Engineering Changes, Deviations and Waivers'.
4. MIL-Std 483 'Configuration Management Practices for Systems, Equipment, Munitions and Computer Programs', 1 June 1971.
5. MIL-Std-490 'Specification Practices', 1 February 1969.
6. MIL-Std-1521B 'Technical Reviews and Audits for Systems, Equipment and Computer Programs'; Military standard; 1985.

INTERNATIONAL

1. IEEE Std-828-1983 'Standard for Software Configuration Management Plans'; Institute of Electrical and Electronic Engineers, 1983.
2. IEEE Std-828-1990 'Standard for Software Configuration Management Plans'; Institute of Electrical and Electronic Engineers, 1990.
3. ANSI/IEEE Std-1042-1987 'Guide to Software Configuration Management'; Institute of Electrical and Electronic Engineers, 1987.
4. ISO 9000-3 'Quality management and quality assurance standards, Part 3: Guidelines for the application of ISO 9001 to the development, supply and maintenance of software'; International Organization for Standardization.

Notes

1. The ISO 9000 series of standards was not originally designed for software, but for manufacturing processes (ISO 9001 covers manufacturing processes which have design aspects). The document referenced above, even though it describes how ISO 9001 is to be used for software, barely mentions Software Configuration Management (paragraph 6.1). The discussion of SCM is less than two pages long and very minimal.

   ISO 9000 and ISO 9001 — the actual standards — do not mention either software or Configuration Management. In software there is no manufacturing process — software is all design. At the time of this writing, the applicability of the ISO 9000 series to software has not been proven.
2. Many organizations, international and national, have standards for Software Configuration Management or standards for software quality/software engineering which contain sections about SCM. However, they are generally beyond the scope of this book. See Chapter 11 for more details.
3. To provide an idea of the quantity of Software Configuration Management standards known, Table A3.1 contains the numbers which have been discovered by this author. It is not possible in this book to cover all of them.

Table A3.1 Software Configuration Management standards

No.	Organization type	Quantity
1	International organizations	2
2	Professional organizations	2
3	Military organizations	4
4	Other professional societies	12
TOTAL		20

Appendix 4

GLOSSARY

Definitions listed in quotation marks and with IEEE at their end denote that the standard IEEE/ANSI definition is used. These are quoted from *IEEE Standard Glossary of Software Engineering Terminology* (the version approved on 15 February 1991).

archive The module archive file in which all evolutionary history of a workfile is retained (see *logfile*).

baseline An agreed-upon release of a product. '(1) A specification or product that has been formally reviewed and agreed upon, that thereafter serves as the basis for further development, and that can be changed only through formal procedures. (2) A document or set of such documents formally designated and fixed at a specific time during the life-cycle of a configuration item.' IEEE.

branch A variant development path that diverges from the primary (trunk) of software development.

CCB A Change Control Board is a committee whose function is to govern the process of change in a project.

configuration control 'An element of Configuration Management, consisting of the evaluation, coordination, approval or disapproval, and implementation of changes to configuration items after formal establishment of their configuration identification.' IEEE.

configuration file A text file that governs the operation of the Software Configuration Management system via configuration parameters and operating conditions.

configuration identification '(1) An element of Configuration Management, consisting of selecting the configuration items for a system and recording their functional and physical characteristics in technical documentation.' IEEE.
(There is a second definition, but it is not relevant in the present context.)

Configuration Management 'A discipline applying technical and administrative direction and surveillance to: identify and document the functional and physical characteristics of a configuration item, control changes to those characteristics, record and report change

161

processing and implementation status, and verify compliance with specified requirements.' IEEE.

configuration status accounting 'An element of Configuration Management, consisting of the recording and reporting of information needed to manage a configuration effectively. This information includes a listing of the approved configuration identification, the status of proposed changes to the configuration and the implementation status of approved changes.' IEEE.

change evaluation cost The number of staff-hours needed to evaluate the requested change, both in technical terms and for possible system-wide effects.

change implementation cost The number of staff-hours needed to fully implement the requested change. In this case, 'fully implement' means updating of all documents and source-code files and full testing (including regression testing) of the updated system/subsystem.

delta The set of differences between one revision of an item and another. Delta reports are usually taken from an archive.

deviation '(1) A departure from a specified requirement. (2) A written authorization, granted prior to the manufacture of an item, to depart from a particular performance or design requirement for a specific number of units or a specific period of time.' IEEE.

error An unexpected, undesired state, situation or value in the document or code.

functional configuration audit (FCA) A management audit which verifies that someone has checked that all functions have been tested against requirements.

hardware The 'touchable', tactile part of a system, usually meant to include the electronics and the mechanical parts of what we are looking at.

item A unique object, to be identified and managed.

lock A semaphore-like marker placed on a particular revision of an item in an archive. If the locked revision is accessed by anyone, a warning is issued and access is prevented. Locks are generally applied when a revision is extracted for updating.

logfile The module archive file in which all evolutionary history of a workfile is retained (see *archive*).

makefile A text file (program) used by the make utility to govern the actions needed to be taken by the make utility to rebuild the system.

make utility A part of the usual set of Configuration Management tools used to automatically and accurately build (and rebuild) a software system.

physical configuration audit (PCA) A management audit, at the end of a development cycle, that verifies the physical presence of all items.

reviewing A technique of displaying results of a development process. The audience will usually consist of fellow developers, managers and user representatives.

revision An instance of a module (or workfile). Each time a workfile is checked back into its archive, its revision number is updated.

software Computer programs and all their constituent parts; e.g. code, requirements and design specifications, user documentation and tests definitions and results.

tip A tip revision is the most recent revision on the trunk of the revision tree or the most recent revision on a branch of the revision tree.

trunk The primary development path of a workfile, as stored in the archive.

variation An alternate form of a module.

version An instance of a (whole) system. May consist of an 'arbitrary slice' through the revisions of the various archives.

workfile A copy of the module for editing or viewing.

Appendix 5

ATTACHMENTS

ATTACHMENT A
CREATE INITIAL BASELINE

Following are several forms which are intended to aid the initial process of setting up the Software Configuration Management system. This, as has been stated, is always a complex process. Try to use your best analyst for this job, and make certain that this person is recognized by the members of the organization as a professional. But, even more significantly, make very certain that this is the staff member who best understands the software process, as performed by your organization!

This attachment begins with a form for startup information gathering. Afterwards, there are several forms, which are intended to be utilized as worksheets, which deal directly with the concerns of security and access control.

Configuration Management Control Form — Project Startup Form

The following form is designed to aid the systems analyst who has been given the task of creating the Software Configuration Management system for the particular project or installation. This means that it is more a Project Startup Form than purely a Software Configuration Management form. (This assumes that the project discussed is that of creating a computerized Software Configuration Management system.)

The objective of the form is to direct the analyst in what is always the first (chronologically) and most difficult problem in the analysis of a complex system — particularly when this particular 'application' is not very well known by the organization. This direction is: 'Exactly what information needs to be "discovered" in order to begin?'

When performing this analysis, the emphasis must be on control. That is, the main analysis objective of the Software Configuration Management system's analyst must be Configuration Management Control. This form has proven to be effective in aiding this objective.

Clearly, this form should be used as a base form. Probably every organization will need to make certain changes, at the very least in the lengths of the various tables.

Configuration Management Control Form

Project Startup Form

Project name: ....

Project/Software Team Leader: ....

Dept. .... Tel. ....

Project Status: ....
 [analysis/requirements, high-level design, detailed design, implementation, testing, production, maintenance]. This list is dependent upon the life-cycle model used by the development organization.

1. Define the development data base usage (estimations):

	No. of files	Disk storage	Bytes/ blocks
Present			
Expected 3 months			
6 months			
9 months			
12 months			

2. Define users of the configuration control system:

User name	User identifica- tion (1–8 char.)	Class

3. Access control for configuration control users:

Structure	User ID	Class (1)	Access control (2)

(1) Classes: Development Team Leader, DBA, Manager, Quality Assurance, User
(2) Access controls: Read, Write, Manager, etc. (the selection must be a function of the security control provided by the tool selected)

4. Startup characteristics of configuration items:

Structure (1)	Scope (2)	Archive (3)	(4)	Compression (5)	Encryption (5)

(1) Include known dependency of this CI to other items
(2) CI scope: local or global
(3) Archive: Y = yes, N = no, NA = not applicable
(4) Archive: location of archive file
(5) Grade on a scale from 0 to 5

5. Project hierarchy/structure (block diagram):

Attach hierarchy charts for system and for each subsystem — as many as are needed to document system hierarchy and configuration item relationships. Note that many items (particularly management documents) are not hierarchically related (most systems when examined from this standpoint are networks).

6. Configuration item (file) entry to data base:

Attach item descriptions for each configuration item.

7. Status reporting (report quantities and distribution):

	Quantity	Distribution
Project/software hierarchy structure report and schema (graphic)		
Items in system report, at all levels		
Users and access authorization report		
Items characteristics report scope, archive, compression, encryption, etc. (see 4, above)		

8. Other instructions:

. . . .

. . . .

. . . .

. . . .

. . . .

ACCESS CONTROL AND SECURITY WORKSHEET

The following worksheets provide guidance for defining and controlling the privileges and permissions of both individuals and groups ('privileges' refers to *how* things are to be performed while 'permissions' refers to *what* the person is allowed). It is important to note that all the concepts being presented here are presented in the 'language' of Intersolv's PVCS — as the system that this book uses for examples. Clearly, any SCM system which one wishes to evaluate for purchase should have equivalent facilities to those discussed here.

Firstly, one should make maximum use of the base facilities of the system. This 'maximum use' probably means that one would wish to use these facilities to define a set of composite facilities to make other definitions clearer.

Begin the process by defining a set of basic privilege levels to be used to define those privileges both for users and for defined groups of users. Notice that most of the privileges defined include one or more of the preceding composite privileges. (This is a sort of 'macro' facility. Very useful!) Note that the 'back-slash' is used as a continuation character.

The following list contains a suggestion for what these macro definitions may look like. Note that there are two 'logical lines' of definitions. The first extends from the most basic AUDITing privileges through some limited updating facility. This represents one logical branch of definitions. This is likely to be used by the less technical staff: i.e. quality assurance, management, testing, secretarial, etc. It is very important to note that many individuals will need to have access to documents, but not to the code (workfiles). This is very common and the SCM system administrator must take this into account.

The second logical line of definitions is more for the developers themselves. It discusses CHANGE, MODIFY and FULLUPDATE privileges. The reasons for developers having different levels of permission might relate to their level of skills or, perhaps, some questions of accessibility which concern product security.

Finally, there is a privilege which combines the facilities of the other two. This is called UNLIMITED and would likely be for a technical project manager. There is also a concept of superuser or ADMINISTRATOR. This privilege is established for the use of the staff member who is responsible for the SCM system.

User Permissions Worksheet
Groups Permissions Worksheet

PRIVILEGE AUDIT: \
  ViewLogfileHeader \ ViewLogfileRev
PRIVILEGE VIEW: \
  AUDIT \ ViewDelta
PRIVILEGE BROWSE: \
  VIEW \ GetTip \ GetNonTip
PRIVILEGE NOUPDATE: \
  LockTip \ BROWSE
PRIVILEGE LIMITEDUPDATE: \
  Unlock \ NOUPDATE \ PutTrunk \ PutBranch \ AddVersion
PRIVILEGE CHANGE: \
  ChangeAccessList \ ChangeOwner \ ChangeProtection \ ChangeCommentDelimiter \
  ChangeWorkfileName
PRIVILEGE MODIFY: \
  CHANGE \ ModifyWorkfileDescription \ ModifyChangeDescription \ ModifyVersion
PRIVILEGE FULLUPDATE: \
  LockNonTip \ StartBranch \ MODIFY \ InitLogfile
PRIVILEGE UNLIMITED: \
  FULLUPDATE \ LIMITEDUPDATE \ Unlock \ BreakLock \ DeleteVersion \
  ModifyVersion \ DeleteRevTip \ DeleteRevNonTip \ ViewAccessDB
PRIVILEGE ADMINISTRATOR: \
  SuperUser
USER MBM (ADMINISTRATOR)
USER MORD (FULLUPDATE)
USER HENRY (LIMITEDUPDATE)
USER SARAH (FULLUPDATE)
USER QA (AUDIT)
USER TESTING (NOUPDATE)
USER SECRETIAL (BROWSE)

ATTACHMENT B
CHANGE REQUEST FORMS

Notes

1. For reasons of brevity, the following three forms use US DOD terminology 'CSCI'. Remember that CSCI, in this context, is simply a synonym for system or subsystem.
2. The following explanations refer to all the three forms which deal with the process of: (a) making a request for a change to be made in a system or item, (b) gaining approval for the change and following up on its outcomes and (c) change notification.

Introductory explanations to the Change Management forms

The forms in this attachment establish a 'standard common method' for beginning the process of requests for changes and continuing the follow-up afterwards.

Paper forms are seldom a necessity. In many installations, the procedures followed demand that these requests begin with such a paper form. Sometimes this form may be something called an engineering change proposal (ECP) form. There are probably other (sometimes, arcane) names. The specific names used are not important: communication is.

In others, the computerized system has been designed to process the requests from the very beginning. When paper forms are needed, these sample forms may be used. They have been tried by many installations and have proven themselves to be very good.

In those cases when paper forms are not used, use these forms as a known strong base from which to begin planning your computerized system. Starting from a known, proven base is always wiser than starting from scratch.

Note that this refers to the beginning of the formal request for a change, but not necessarily the actual start of the process of change. This process of change may have begun from any of several kinds of formal or informal inputs, such as an error or trouble report (quite formally reported or, at least, well documented) or a fresh, original idea from one or more of the project's personnel.

Whatever form is chosen to be used by the organization, the originator of the change request must be required to fill in the change request form as per accepted standards.

The role of the product assurance representation

All change requests which are submitted to the project should be reviewed by a representative of product assurance or whichever member of the staff is delegated by the product assurance function. This preliminary review is intended to validate the change request submittal.

The product assurance representative performs checks upon the CR forms to ensure validity. All validity checks should be documented in the change log. A CR validity check should include, at least, the following:

- Assurance that a sufficiency of documentation for the successful processing of the change has been supplied.
- Assurance that the author/originator of the change proposal has been authorized to submit change proposals. Authorization to submit the change proposals is frequently

limited: some organizations allow anyone to submit proposals; others limit this function to qualified or authorized personnel.

- If the change request began from a problem report, the recreatability of the problem by development personnel must be ensured — this requirement is linked to the documentation mentioned by the first requirement, listed above.
- Ascertaining that this request has not been previously processed (perhaps, from a different source).

The log of the change requests should be maintained by the product assurance representative or whoever is serving the organization as the person responsible to the Change Control Board. In this way, unique numbering of each change request is ensured. This author also very strongly suggests that this log be automated and computerized.

Change request scope

The change request should refer to a specific system function, software component (module/CSC) or subsystem (CSCI). That is, a specific configuration item. All additional components which are affected — whether these are managerial or user documentation, technical items or code — must have all known or estimated details concerning this effect documented on the CR form.

The project, product or plant Software Configuration Management 'group' is responsible for the function of updating the version/edition numbers of the component/CSC (or subsystem/CSCI). Generally, this act is performed by the Software Configuration Management system software. In any case, no other party is allowed to update these identifications and all responsibility resides with this organizational function.

Change authorization

With the exception of any special, well documented circumstances, all changes must be properly authorized before implementation. This authorization should be signed-off by the residing chair of the Change Control Board.

Implementation activities are performed by the appropriate technical authority. After implementation, all affected configuration items are submitted for testing and quality assurance. (In the case of CIs which are documents, replace the phrase 'submitted for testing' with 'submitted for reviewing'.)

All follow-up activities are performed by, or are the responsibility of, software quality assurance (officially, the Change Control Board coordinator). The change authorization always includes all affected documents.

To reduce project risk as much as possible, no change should be authorized for implementation unless viable alternatives have been evaluated.

Software Change Request

Security: _ _ _ _ _ _ _ _ _ _ _

Change No.: _ _ _ _ _   Date: _ _ _ _ _ _ _   Page _ _ _ of _ _ _
Project: _ _ _ _ _ _ _ _ _ _   Change Name: _ _ _ _ _ _ _ _

Reason for Change: ☐   1. Requirement Change   2. Design Change
3. Error Discovered   4. Quality Assurance

Change Description: _
_ _
_ _
_ _
_ _

CSCIs Involved in Change

Cost of evaluation: _ _ _ _ _ _ _ _ _ _ hours   Cost to implement: _ _ _ _ _ _ _ _ _ _ _ _ hours

CSCI Identification	Documentation Affected								
	Req	TLD	DD	Code	Test	ICD			
	Req	TLD	DD	Code	Test	ICD			
	Req	TLD	DD	Code	Test	ICD			
	Req	TLD	DD	Code	Test	ICD			

Alternative Solution: _
_ _
_ _

Comments: _
_ _
_ _

SCCB Decision: Request Denied   Date: _ _ _ _ _ _ _ _ _ _ _ _ _
To be Evaluated   Name: _ _ _ _ _ _ _ _ _ _ _
Request Frozen   Signature: _ _ _ _ _ _ _ _ _

Comments: _
_ _
_ _

Software Change Authorization

Security: _ _ _ _ _ _ _ _ _ _ _

Change No.: _ _ _ _ _	Date: _ _ _ _ _ _ _	Page _ _ _ of _ _ _
Project: _ _ _ _ _ _ _ _ _ _	Change Name: _ _ _ _ _ _ _	

Changes to be Implemented

No.	SCR +	SPR +	Responsible	Data Due	SCN*	SCN Date*

+ use either SCR or SPR reference for each change
* filled in when SCN is completed

CSCIs involved in Change

CSCI Identification	Documentation Affected								
	Req	TLD	DD	Code	Test	ICD			
	Req	TLD	DD	Code	Test	ICD			
	Req	TLD	DD	Code	Test	ICD			
	Req	TLD	DD	Code	Test	ICD			

Comments: _
_ _
_ _
_ _
_ _

Approved by: _ _ _ _ _ _ _ _ _ _ _ _ _ _ _ _ _ _ _	Date: _ _ _ _ _ _ _ _ _ _
SCCB Approval: Name: _ _ _ _ _ _ _ _ _ _ _ _ _ _ _	Date: _ _ _ _ _ _ _ _ _ _
Signature: _	

Software Change Notice

Security: _ _ _ _ _ _ _ _ _ _

Change No.: _ _ _ _ _ _	Date: _ _ _ _ _ _ _	Page _ _ _ of _ _ _
Project: _ _ _ _ _ _ _ _ _ _	Change Name: _ _ _ _ _ _ _ _	

Changes Implemented

No.	Implementation Status	Responsible	Date

Software/Documentation Revision Changes

Software/Document Identification	Prior Change	After Change

Comments: _
_ _
_ _
_ _
_ _

Approved by: _ _ _ _ _ _ _ _ _ _ _ _ _ _ _ _ _	Date: _ _ _ _ _ _ _ _ _ _ _ _ _ _
Title: _	Signature: _ _ _ _ _ _ _ _ _ _ _ _ _

SCCB Approval: Name: _ _ _ _ _ _ _ _ _ _ _ _ _ _ _ _ _	Date: _ _ _ _ _ _ _
Signature: _ _ _ _ _ _ _ _ _ _ _ _ _ _ _	

Received By CM: Name: _ _ _ _ _ _ _ _ _ _ _ _ _ _ _ _ _	Date: _ _ _ _ _ _ _

Change Control Board/change request interaction

This suggested procedure is to be followed by the Change Control Board.

This is not intended to comprehensively define Change Control Board activities. For a comprehensive procedure, see the appropriate section of the book.

The documentation of the change request (CR) should be updated by the Change Control Board (CCB), as events occur. This update should include all information gathered by the evaluation and by the implementation processes. This information should always include any expected costs of the change(s).

This information must always be established before change authorization. Project management and the originator of the change request should be notified of the expected costs of implementation of the change, before authorization of the change's implementation.

ATTACHMENT C
SOFTWARE PROBLEM REPORTING PROCEDURE

The following flow chart, with its accompanying explanatory tables, represents the process of software problem reporting. It is important to note two points: the information flows that this process must deal with (outlined in Table A5.1) and the various 'states' that a software problem report may exist in (Table A5.2).

The process of software problem reporting creates and moves ten kinds of information. The flow chart graphically describes the sources and destinations of these information objects.

Obviously, the most basic item of information is evidence that the problem has been discovered. This is called 'problem documentation' and must include as much evidence as possible so that those responsible may be able to properly deal with the problem. This directly results in either an 'invalid SPR' or a 'valid SPR'. If everything is agreed upon, then a change request will be created from the SPR (providing, of course, that it has been validated). Occasionally, a valid SPR may generate a 'non-implementable change.' When this happens, clearly the initiator of the change must be notified. If the change is implementable, this is only knowable after the change request has been properly evaluated; an 'evaluated CR' is then moved along for processing by the developers. At this point, a change authorization must be issued to development, to allow them to begin work. This is the equivalent of a work order in other industries. The developers issue an implementation note to inform the quality assurance and testers to prepare themselves for the coming jobs of verification and validation of the change being performed. 'Test results' are one of the objects which result from this process. After the change has been implemented and tested, a change notification will be issued to notify that this event has been completed.

Certainly, in small organizations, some of this may not be needed. Just as, in very large, complex projects, there may be a need for more than this. The Software Configuration Management function, together with the quality assurance function, must prepare this procedure. It must be validated by management and by development.

Software Problem Reporting Procedure Flow Chart

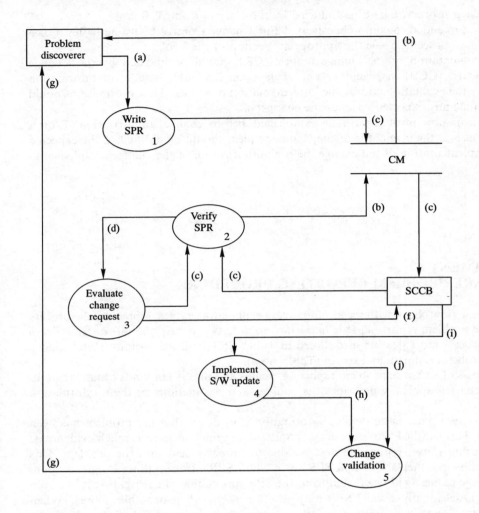

Table A5.1 provides the keys to the data flows (arrows) in the flow chart. Table A5.2 outlines the possible state for a software problem report.

Table A5.1   Data flows in problem report processing

(a)   Problem documentation
(b)   Invalid SPR
(c)   SPR
(d)   Change request (CR)
(e)   Non-implementable change
(f)   Evaluated CR
(g)   Change notification
(h)   Implementation note
(i)   Change authorization
(j)   Test results

Table A5.2   SPR states

1. Written
2. Invalid
3. Validated
   A validated SPR is transformed into a change request (CR)

ATTACHMENT D
SOFTWARE CONFIGURATION MANAGEMENT PROCESS
EVALUATION FORMS

Software Configuration Management Evaluation Form

Copy		Document Type	Page	of	Security	Document Number
		Checklist			unlimited	QA _ 5901/Q2
DOCUMENT TITLE		**Software Configuration Management Evaluation**				
BASED UPON DID						
Issue History		First Issue Date			Current Issue Date	Version
		1 July 1988			19 Jan 1992	2.4

	Reviewer	Approved	Approved	Configuration Management	Product Assurance
Name					
Sign					
Date					

Review Type	Audit Number	CSCI Number

Project Name: _____
_____
CSCI Name: _____
_____
Supplier: _____
_____

Conclusions / Recommendations: _____
_____
_____
_____

EVALUATION RESULTS SCORING FORM

		Perfect Score	Actual Score	Per cent Comply
1	**Scope**			
1.1	Identification	2		
1.2	Purpose	2		
1.3	Introduction	4		
	Subtotals	8		
2	**Referenced documents**	2		
	Subtotals	2		
3	**Configuration identification**			
3.1	Nomenclature	6		
3.2	Documentation	6		
3.3	Media	5		
3.4	Computer software configuration items (CSCIs)	7		
3.5	Revision/Version identities	6		
	Subtotals	30		
4	**Configuration control**			
4.1	Functional baseline	3		
4.2	Allocated baseline	2		
4.3	Prior to preliminary design review (PDR)	3		
4.4	Prior to critical design review (CDR)	3		
4.5	Coding, testing and integration	2		
4.6	CSCI release	4		
4.7	Access control	2		
4.8	Change control	3		
4.9	Deviations and waivers	3		
4.10	Trouble report control	2		
	Subtotals	27		
5	**Configuration status accounting**			
5.1	Status	2		
5.2	Traceability	1		
	Subtotals	3		
	TOTALS	**70**		

Appendix 6

A BRIEF GUIDE TO THE PVCS COMMAND SET

This appendix provides a 'taxonomy' of a typical software system product, devoted to the task of Software Configuration Management. 'Typical' in this sense mostly means that system which is the most common. This, as has been stated above, probably means the PVCS toolset.

Historically, the Source Code Control System (SCCS), from Bell Laboratories might have more installations than PVCS. Because the SCCS software package is distributed free of charge, neither the actual number of installations or, even more so, the number of users, can ever be known or knowable. However, a more accurate evaluation of this concept of 'typicality' must be based upon a product that people take because they actually want it, not because it happens to be there.

Every professional knows that *free* is not necessarily the cheapest option. Very few users actually use SCCS. Even fewer of those use it from choice. Clearly, PVCS is the most widely used (commercial) product — despite the fact that it is still very far from being our ideal of the *perfect* SCM system. Very far from it!

One can readily see from this list of commands that there are aspects of SCM which the product covers quite well. A detailed examination will also show that there are aspects which it does not cover at all. These aspects must either be developed in-house (some sort of application envelope) or passed-over by the organization. Our research has found that functionality of the PVCS system is reasonably advanced *vis-à-vis* the marketplace.

This appendix is not intended to have any commercial aspect. Not all of the system's commands are listed here — for instance, the system directives are not described, though they are quite important for the setup of the system. This is also not intended to be a user's guide, of any sort. The commands which have been included are those which this author thinks the reader will find of interest (accurate to version 5.1 of the software, which was released in the second quarter of 1993).

The appendix includes (selectively) both explanations and comments. However, there has also been an effort to keep these as short as possible. The general section, at the beginning, is to aid overall understanding of what comes later. It is not really critical to the central task.

GENERAL

File specifications (both archive and workfile specifications)

- There are various basic ways to specify a file.
- The processing time (resource usage) is very dependent upon the specification method chosen.
- The user may use standard 'wild card' characters as much as is needed. This is very advantageous.

[drive:]filename.c-v(filename.c)

- – One may specify the filename simply. PVCS will compute whether it is a workfile or an archive.
  – One may specify a workfile by typing the name in parentheses.
  – One may specify both an archive and a workfile, concatenated; the workfile is written in parentheses:
  C:\filedir(filename.c).
  – There is no ambiguity. No computation is required to determine either filename.
- The directory of the archive corresponding to FILENAME.C is to be found in FILEDIR. FILENAME.C-V must live in FILEDIR.

filename.c

- PVCS will spend a significant amount of time discovering whether FILENAME.C is an archive or a workfile.

filename.c-v

- PVCS knows that the filename refers to an archive. The name of the working file is computed from the name of the archive.

(filename.c)

- Because of the parentheses, PVCS knows that the filename refers to a workfile.

Revision specification

- By unspecified number   *Latest revision*
- Major number only   *Latest revision with major number*
- Branch number   *Latest revision on that branch*
- Major and minor numbers   *Exactly that revision*
- Number consists of:
  Number (major — 'm')
  'm.n'
  Number (minor — 'n')
  Range from 0 to 65535
  The -r option is used to be specific

- Symbolic system version label
  Version specification
  -v < version label >
  -r\< version label >
  Use quotation marks with spaces or tabs
  Version labels
  Identify specific revisions
  Alphanumeric string
  Case sensitive
  Use quotation marks with spaces or tabs
- Time and/or date

PVCS KEYWORDS

- Embed *Who?*, *What?*, *When?*, *Where?*, *Why?* information in a module
  $Revision: 3.3 $ The revision number
  $Date: 24 Feb. 1993 10:28:06 $ The check-in date of a revision
  $Author: MBM $ Who checked the revision in
  $Header: C:/WM45/BOOKS/CM/CM12.WMV 3.3 24 Feb. 1993 10:28:06 MBM $
  $Log: C:/WM45/BOOKS/CM/CM12.WMV $ Rev 3.3 24 Feb. 1993 10:28:06 MBM
  $Modtime: 24 Feb. 1993 08:46:06 $ Time of last modification
  $Workfile: CM12.WMR $ The stored file's name
  $Archive: C:/WM45/BOOKS/CM/CM12.WMV $ The full pathname of the archive

PVCS COMMANDS, COMMON OPTIONS

- -c < configuration file >
  Causes the named (alternate) configuration file to be processed instead of the normal or default configuration file. If no filename is specified no configuration file at all is read.
      This option, if used, must be the first option given on the command line for the GET command.
- @ < command file >
  Read command file for additional options.
  Accomplished prior to reading the remainder of the command line.
  Arbitrary nesting depth.
- -n
  Implies a negative response to any query that the associated command may make.
- -y
  Implies an affirmative response to any query that the associated command may make.
- -h
  Causes the display of on-line help information regarding the function of the command entered, including its syntax and available options.
      Program execution terminates after the help information is displayed regardless of additional parameters specified.

- -q[o]
  Specifies the quiet mode of operation. Only error conditions are reported. Implicit '-y' option unless either '-n' specified or '-qo', quiet only, is used.
- -r < revision number or version label >
  Specifies revision or version to be operated upon. Absence of this argument implies that the latest trunk revision (the TIP revision) is to be used.
- -v < version label >
  Specifies the version of the system to be operated upon.

GET

File specification additions:
- FILENAME.C-V(C:\TESTDIR)
  The file is checked out and placed in the specified directory. The directory specification may optionally contain a disk drive specifier, a pathname, or both. Wild card characters may be used.
- FILENAME.C-V(C:\TESTDIR\NEWFILE.C)
  The workfile is placed in the specified directory with the specified name. The pathname and disk drive specifiers are optional.

get[< options >] < filelist >

Retrieves a revision from one or more archives.
- -l[< revision >]
  Specifies that the named revision should be locked with current VCSID.
     If the specified revision is already locked, or the user already has another revision locked, a message will be displayed and GET may abort. If no revision is given, the latest trunk revision is assumed. If the revision is specified with a branch number, the latest revision on that branch is assumed.
     This option is used when the user wishes to edit or otherwise modify the file. Once the revision is locked, no other user may GET that revision for editing or modification purposes, unless this option has been specifically allowed.
- -d < date/time specification >
  Checks out the latest revision that was checked in no later than the specified date/time.
- -p[< revision >]
  Pipe the checked out revision to standard output, rather than creation of the corresponding workfile.
- -u
  The update option causes PVCS to check out a workfile only if the revision to be checked out has a later date/time stamp than the existing workfile.
     This option is useful for updating a set of files to ensure that the latest revisions are present. This option works on both locking and non-locking GETs and should be used advisedly for special situations.
- -s < suffix template >
  Specifies a suffix template (the suffix, refers to the file's extension, the command refers to the method of calculating how the extension is to be changed between the workfile and the archive). Overrides current setting of LOGSUFFIX.

- -t[< revision >]
  Specifies that the checked-out file should have its date/time stamp set to the current time. If this option is not specified, PVCS will set the file date/time stamp to the time that the file was last modified.
  This option is equivalent to doing a 'touch' command on the checked-out file.
- -w[< revision >]
  This option specifies that the checked-out workfile should be writable irrespective of the protection level and lock status of the archive. This option does not affect the lock status of any revision.

PUT

- PUT stores a new revision in a archive. If the archive does not exist and AUTOCREATE is set, then PUT will create the archive.
  If lock checking is enabled, the predecessor revision must be locked by the name VCSID.
  Unless '-m' is specified, the user will be prompted for a description of the changes made to the revision.
  If the new revision is identical to the predecessor, PUT will query the user to confirm the installation of a new revision.

Possible queries

- Should unchanged workfiles be checked in?
- Should a file with a time stamp older than parent be checked in anyway?
- Should a version label identical to the new version label be deleted?

IDENT

- IDENT [< options >] < filelist >
- IDENT examines the specified file list for keywords and prints those keywords found, to standard output. This is useful in determining what the revision number of a particular module is. The < filelist > may be source, object or executable code, libraries, archives, or any other file type.
- Only the @ and -h options apply to this command.

REGEN

- REGEN applies editing instructions, contained in a delta file, to a reference file to regenerate a target file which is written to standard output. The delta file is commonly generated by the VDIFF command.
- Only the @ and -h options are appropriate and recognized.

VCS

- -a[< vcsid list >]
  Adds < vcsid list > to the current access list of the specified archive(s). If < vcsid list > is omitted, all names are removed from the access list of the specified archive(s).
  When creating an archive with VCS, this option specifies an access list to be associated with the archive. The access list specified in the configuration file is ignored.
- vcs[< options >] < filelist >
  VCS performs several administrative functions on archives, such as creating new archives or modifying existing ones.
  An archive consists of:
  - zero or more revisions of a workfile
  - descriptions of the revisions made to the workfile
  - a description of the purpose of the workfile and parameters controlling the handling of the archive
- -i
  Creates and initializes an archive containing no revision. If the archive already exists, permission is required to overwrite the archive. If permission is not implicit in any other options selected, the user is prompted to either give or deny permission.
  A description of the workfile contained in the archive is requested. The < filelist > parameter must specify the name of the workfile. When using this option, the options -l, -u, -v and -w are ignored.
- -ec < string >
  Specifies that the comment prefix used in keyword expansion be changed to < string >. Omission of the < string > parameter causes no comment prefix to be used.
- -en
  Disable keyword expansion in the archive.
- -ey
  Enable keyword expansion in the archive.
- -m[< text >]
  This option identifies text used to replace a change description in the archive. Omission of < text > causes an editor to be invoked unless standard input has been redirected.
- m@[< filename >]
  The new text is taken from < filename >.
  If < filename > is omitted, MESSAGESUFFIX is used to compute the filename.
- -l[< revision >]
  Locks the specified revision. If no revision is specified, locks the latest trunk revision. If the revision is specified by branch number, the latest revision on the branch is locked.
- -u[< revision >]
  Unlocks the specified revision. If no revision is specified, unlocks the only revision locked by < user >.
  If the revision is specified by major number only, the latest revision having that major number is unlocked. If the specified revision is locked by another VCSID, the user will be asked to confirm the lock breaking (providing that this user has the access rights) unless -q, -n or -y options are also given.
- -p[e][k][l][t][w]
- + p[e][k][l][t][w]

Modifies the protection of the archive (both of them):
- removes the specified protection
+ adds it

- -o[< owner vcsid >]
  Changes the owner of the specified archive(s) to < owner vcsid >. If < owner vcsid > is not given, the owner is set to null.

- -s < suffix template >
  Specifies the suffix template to use instead of the current LOGSUFFIX in computing archive names.

- -v < version label >[< revision number/version label >]
  Associates the symbolic < version label > with the revision specified by < revision number/version label >. If no < revision number/version label > is specified, the latest trunk revision is assumed.

  If the version label already exists, permission to override is required unless the -q, -y or -n options are also specified.

- -t[< text >]
  Specifies text describing the workfile when initializing an archive. Replaces any existing descriptive text. Omitting < text > parameter invokes an editor unless redirection from standard input is accomplished.

- -t@[< filename >]
  Take the descriptive text from < filename >. If < filename > is not specified, compute the filename from MESSAGESUFFIX.

- -w < workfile name >
  Allows the workfile name, stored in the archive, to be changed. This is useful if it becomes desirable to rename the archive. The -w option allows you to make a corresponding change to the name of the workfile.

- -v < new revision label > :: < old version label >
  Change < old version label > to < new version label > in specified archive(s).

- -v < version label > : DELETE
  The version label < version label > is deleted from the archive.

Possible queries

- Should the existing file be overwritten when creating an archive?
- Should a previous version label that is identical to the new version label be deleted?

VDEL

- VDEL [< options >] < filelist >
  Deletes revision from archives
  Tip revision = changes lost
  Any other revision, changes not lost
  Change history lost

- -r < revision range >
  The -r option specifies the revisions to be deleted from the archive. The range of revisions can be specified in the following ways:

< revision >	Specific revision
* < revision >	Up to and including
< revision > *	This and all following (branch)
< rev > * < rev >	Inclusive range (branch)

VDIFF

- VDIFF [< options >] < reference >   < target > [< deltas >]
- VDIFF compares two files, the reference file and the target file, and reports the differences between them. The difference is displayed in terms of how the first file is changed to produce the second. Optionally, VDIFF can generate a delta script that can be used to regenerate the target file from the reference file or copies thereof.
- -t
Specifies the test mode of operation. Under test mode, no differences are displayed. Instead, the return value of VDIFF is used to determine the equality of the files. A return code of 0 means that no differences were detected.
- -d
- This option causes VDIFF to print a delta script to the standard output device. The script file contains edit commands used by the REGEN command to generate the target file from the reference file. Output may be redirected to a file.
- -e < number >
Specifies the number of columns between tab stops for tab.

VJOURNAL

- VJOURNAL [< options >] < journal file(s) >
The VJOURNAL command is used to view portions of PVCS journal files selectively. A journal file is a text file in which PVCS commands make notes about modifications made to PVCS archives. This provides project administrators with an AUDIT TRAIL from which they can determine who did what to which file and when it was done. The journal file is a normal text file.
- -d < date range >
Allows the user to specify a range of dates or times for the journal entries to be displayed.
- -l < archive list >
This option specifies a comma-separated list of the names of PVCS journal files for which a report is desired.
- -o < operation list >
This option specifies a comma-separated list of PVCS commands of interest. Recognized operations are GET, PUT and VCS. Only those journal entries made as a result of operations on the list will be output.
- -u < user list >
This option specifies a comma-separated list of PVCS user names (VCSIDs) of interest. Only those journal entries attributed to one of the names on the list will be displayed.

VLOG

- -a < author list >
Causes VLOG to display only revisions stored by users whose VCSIDs are specified in the comma-separated author list.
- -o < owner list >
Display information only for archives whose owner's VCSID is listed in the comma-separated owner list of VCSIDs.
- -b
Specifies 'brief output' and will only display information about the archive itself. Information about individual revisions is omitted.
- -bn[branch]
Produces a one-line report naming the newest revision on the specified branch. If no branch is specified, the trunk is assumed.
- -d < date range >
Causes VLOG to limit its display to only those revisions checked in within the specified date range.
- -l[< locker list >]
Display information only for the (explicitly or ambiguously) specified archives that are currently locked. The < locker list > is a comma-separated list of VCSIDs. If locker list is specified, only those revisions locked by a member of the list are displayed.
- -bl[< locker list >]
Produces an extremely brief report giving only the archive name, locker VCSID and revisions locked. If the locker list is supplied, the report is limited to revisions locked by a VCSID found in the locker list. The VCSIDs in the locker list are separated only by commas.
- -br[< revision or branch >]
Produces a report that contains only information about the revisions. Information about the archive itself, such as headed or attribute information, is not included.
- -bv < version label >
- Displays the revision numbers corresponding to the specified version label in each specified archive. This provides a convenient way to obtain a list of revision numbers that are associated with a given version label.
- -w < suffix template >
Specifies the suffix template to be used to derive archive names from workfile names. This option overrides the LOGSUFFIX configuration parameter.
- -r < revision or revision range >
Displays information about the specified revision or revision range only. The range may be specified in the following ways:
< revision >	Specific revision
* < revision >	Up to and including
< revision > *	This and all following (branch)
< rev > * < rev >	Inclusive range (branch)

VMRG

- VMRG [<options>] <basefile> <file1> <file2>
  VMRG compares two files to a common ancestor and combines the changes they represent into a single new revision. VMRG notes the changes made to the ancestor or <basefile> to derive <file1> and then performs the same changes on <file2>. By default <file2> becomes the 'merge file' and is overwritten. You may avoid overwriting <file2> by directing output to the standard output device.

  If an area of <basefile> was changed in both <file1> and <file2>, both sets of changes are output to the merge file and the possible conflicts flagged.
- <file2>
  Specified as workfile. Must be present on disk.
- -p
  Write the merged file to standard output device.
- -s <log suffix template>
  Specifies the suffix template to be used to derive archive names from workfile names. This option overrides the LOGSUFFIX configuration parameter.

EXHIBITS

FOR A SOFTWARE CONFIGURATION MANAGEMENT COURSE

EXHIBIT 1

CONFIGURATION MANAGEMENT DEFINITION

Configuration Management is a process for efficiently developing and maintaining software by improving:

- Accountability
- Reproducibility
- Traceability
- Coordination

EXHIBIT 2

A GENERAL CONFIGURATION MANAGEMENT DEFINITION

Configuration Management is a management discipline which:

1. Identifies the proposed or implemented configuration of a system at discrete points in time
2. Systematically records and traces changes to all system components

for purposes of assuring:

- Integrity, accountability, visibility reproducibility, project coordination and traceability
- Formal control of system/product evolution

EXHIBIT 3

A CONFIGURATION IS A LIST OF PARTS, AND THEIR RELATIVE ARRANGEMENT

The configuration of *our* system is the exact (well defined) list of all parts used, their relative arrangement and the methods to be used to construct our system from these parts.

EXHIBIT 4

SOFTWARE IS:

- Structured information with:
  - Hierarchical
  - Logical
  - Functional
  properties

created as text

- Machine 'procurable' in its most advanced state
- Maintained in various forms during development, use and operations

Therefore:

- A software configuration is a well defined arrangement of software parts and the *exact* procedure(s) to be used for reconstructing it.
- This *must* also include procedures for reconstructing previous versions and/or releases.

EXHIBIT 5

SOFTWARE CONFIGURATION MANAGEMENT

- Most importantly, addresses three of the most critical problems facing any development and/or maintenance project involving multiple developers.
- These are the problems of shared data, double maintenance and simultaneous updates.

EXHIBIT 6

SOFTWARE CONFIGURATION MANAGEMENT

is always performed

Sometimes it is manual and sometimes computerized.
What are the differences?

Automated vs. manual CM

Automatic	Manual
Good for:	Good for:
large projects	human judgement
ensuring compliance	
Bad for:	Bad for:
sophisticated judgements	heavy use
	many loopholes

EXHIBIT 7

TAXONOMY

Software Configuration Management (SCM) is composed of exactly four activities or parts:

>   Identification
>   Control
>   Status accounting
>   Auditing

In the terminology used by the IEEE standards, these are:

- Identification   (SCI)   3.1 of SCMP
- Control   (SCC)   3.2 of SCMP
- Status accounting   (SCSA)   3.3 of SCMP
- Auditing   (SCA)   3.4 of SCMP

EXHIBIT 8

TRACEABILITY

is the ability to link individual events and parts to each other, in time.

Remember!
All parts have events — all events have parts!

EXHIBIT 9

SOFTWARE CONFIGURATION IDENTIFICATION

- defines 'granularity' of CM
- defines what is needed to be seen
- assures that the identification scheme reflects the structure of the
  - product
  - project
  - organization

It is a critical project management task

EXHIBIT 10

EXAMPLES OF ITEMS TO BE IDENTIFIED

Names:

- variables source code
- programs/procedures
- files object code
- EPROMs/media command files
- test data requirements
- design details/objects
- user documentation

Terminology:

- CPCIs
- BoM — Bill of 'materials'
- WBS — Work breakdown structure
- Versions/baselines

EXHIBIT 11

SOFTWARE PARTS

Software parts will typically be:

- Requirements specifications
- Design/interface specifications
- Test designs
- Plans, such as: SQAP, SCMP, SVVP
- A code module (source or object)

Or they may be:

- Individual keystrokes
- A single line in a COBOL program
- Any identifiable item

A software part is the 'smallest piece' of software which you are going to want to manage.

EXHIBIT 12

VISIBILITY

Visibility means:

- Permitting the software to be seen by anyone who is allowed to see it. Permitting management to 'see' what is happening and permitting management to be seen on a project; that is, permitting them to really manage.

EXHIBIT 13

IMPORTANT IDENTIFICATION PRINCIPLES

- Software products are labelled at discrete points in time.
- Each product label is related to the label of all predecessors.
- One organization performs labelling throughout the life-cycle.
- Partitioning a baseline is always subjective.
- Create some partition and maintain it.
- Baselines live forever.

EXHIBIT 14

IDENTIFY PROJECT BASELINES

- Baselines integrate groups together.
- Construction of aggregates is described.
- Each 'build' has an individual baseline.
- Once an item is tied into a baseline, changes are made only via CCB.
- Each release (major or minor) is a baseline.
- Baselines define the state of the system in time.

EXHIBIT 15

_____

DELINEATE PROJECT TITLING, LABELLING AND NUMBERING

Can be via numbers/mnemonic hierarchy

For embedded S/W:

- ([EP]ROM) media need to be linked with software and 'versioned'.

_____

EXHIBIT 16

_____

REVISION IDENTIFICATION

- Numeric — normally start at 1.0
- Automatic — computation of next number
- Can be manually overridden — within reason
- Branch revisions can be identified (1.2.3.4)

_____

EXHIBIT 17

_____

VERSION IDENTIFICATION

Purpose:

- Identifies an instance of the system
- Provides project milestones
- Software life-cycle performed 'naturally'
- Release levels
- Working revisions
- Exact and unique mapping between version label and module revisions
- Each version unique
- A version is linked to a specific instance of a revision
- A revision may have many version labels

_____

EXHIBIT 18

SOFTWARE CONFIGURATION CONTROL

What is control?
1. Define scheme to relate file identification to document identification.
2. Define scheme to relate S/W identification to H/W identification.
3. Define third party S/W identification scheme and how to enforce it.
4. Define scheme for reused or reusable S/W.
5. Define identification scheme for support software.

EXHIBIT 19

CONFIGURATION CONTROL

- Levels of control must be defined.
- What you identified you must control.
- Responsibilities should have been defined.
- levels of authority may change for different CPCIs (subsystems).
- Source of change may affect authority.

EXHIBIT 20

SUPPORT ELEMENTS NEEDED

- Tools for CC
- Change control
- Procedure for requesting change
- CCB

EXHIBIT 21

CHANGE IS THE INDUSTRY LIFE-BLOOD

Evolutionary change
Growth of a system through control — by orderly
management planning

Revolutionary change
The unexpected or unplanned modification of a system
software configuration control

EXHIBIT 22

SOFTWARE CONFIGURATION CONTROL

The tools and techniques via which management orchestrates all the processes by which
the software portion of a system achieves and maintains a visible structure (components
and relationships) throughout the system life-cycle.

EXHIBIT 23

THE SHARED DATA PROBLEM

Situation
Several programmers or projects share common modules of code, documentation,
specifications.

Problem:
A bug is created in Project A, in the common code. Project B discovers a new bug.
- Who changed which Project B module?
- Who changed common code?
- What changes have been made lately?

NOBODY KNOWS!

EXHIBIT 24

CREATING THE PROBLEM

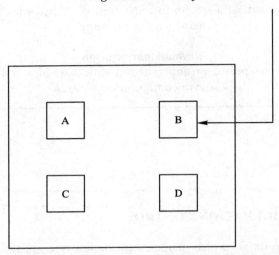

Programmer 1 modifies module B

EXHIBIT 25

DISCOVERING THE PROBLEM

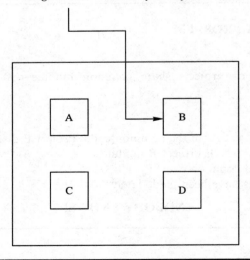

Programmer 2 has a system failure

EXHIBIT 26

SOLVING THE PROBLEM

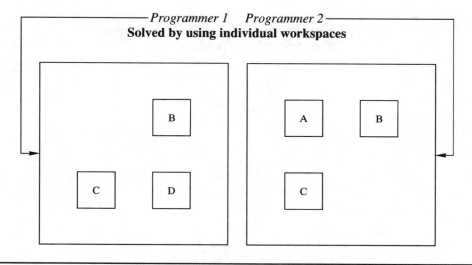

Programmer 1   Programmer 2
Solved by using individual workspaces

EXHIBIT 27

THE DOUBLE MAINTENANCE PROBLEM

Situation
A module is common to several projects.
Each programmer retains his or her 'personal' copy.

Problem
When a problem is discovered, who is responsible for coordinating the fix in all copies?
Can a 'where used' list be created?

EXHIBIT 28

DEFINING THE SITUATION

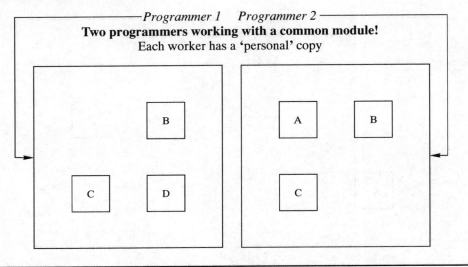

EXHIBIT 29

ONE OF THEM HAS A 'TASK'

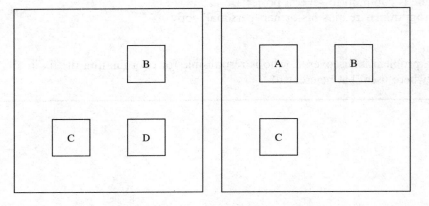

EXHIBIT 30

2's TASK MAY CREATE 1's PROBLEM!

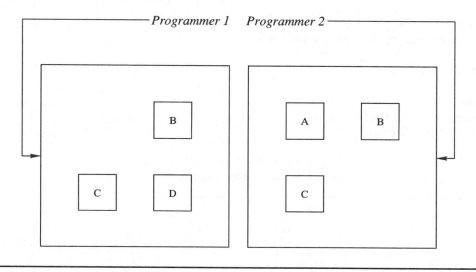

EXHIBIT 31

LACK OF COORDINATION — CRASH!!!

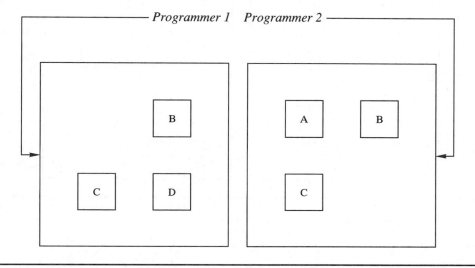

EXHIBIT 32

THE SIMULTANEOUS UPDATE PROBLEM

Situation
Two (or more) programmers are assigned to a certain project.
They share a single program file.
Each has their own copy.

Problem
Programmer A 'checks in' the file.
Programmer B 'checks in' the file.

Programmer 'B' has now destroyed
the work performed by Programmer A!

EXHIBIT 33

EVERYONE HAS A PERSONAL COPY OF 'B'

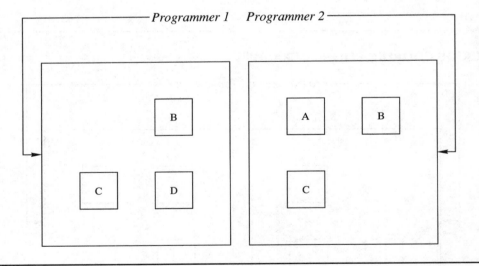

EXHIBIT 34

PROGRAMMER '1' CHECKS IN 'B'

Since everyone is very organized, when Programmer 1's task is finished all modules are checked in — including, of course, 'B'.

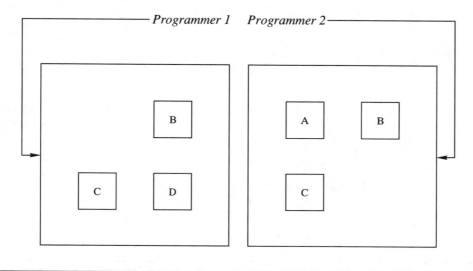

EXHIBIT 35

PROGRAMMER '2' CHECKS IN 'B'

The whole organization is disciplined; Programmer '2' also checks in everything — including 'B'

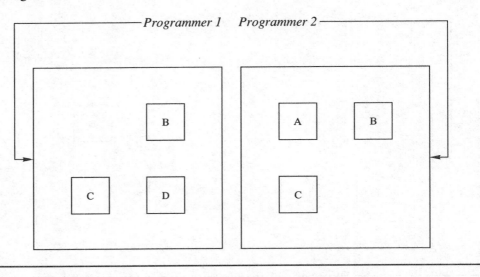

EXHIBIT 36

_____

THE FIRST ITERATION IS OVERWRITTEN!

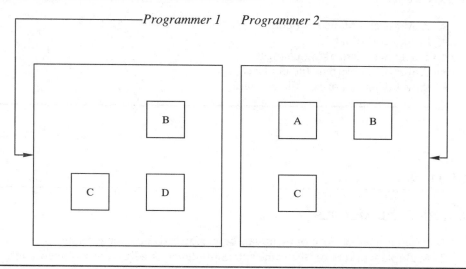

_____

EXHIBIT 37

_____

BENEFITS OF AUTOMATED S/W CM

Helps prevent:
- Lack of information about changes
- Recurrence of bugs ('I fixed that one already!')
- Confusion from conflicting changes
- Unauthorized change
- Difficulties in reconstructing old versions
- Incomplete or inaccurate build attempts

HELPS PREVENT SURPRISES!

_____

EXHIBIT 38

FILE LOCKING

- Prevents simultaneous update
- Forces coordination
- Tracks who is making changes
- Prevents inadvertent file changes
- Prevents unauthorized file changes

EXHIBIT 39

BRANCHES AND MERGES

1. Parallel lines of development can be performed for later merging.
2. Multiple workers on the same file. Simultaneous edits can be joined later.
3. Multiple, emergency bug repairs which can be 'folded in' later.

EXHIBIT 40

CHANGE PROCESSING AND CONTROL

The processing of changes
1. No single procedure can cover all levels of change and approval. That means that the procedure must have means for ad hoc modifications.
2. Define information needed for approval.
3. Identify the routing of the various types of requests.
4. Describe the controls to be used for all libraries.
5. Describe the procedure(s) to be used for implementing changes to code, specifications, documentation, etc.

IN-HOUSE OR IN THE 'FIELD'

EXHIBIT 41

CHANGE HISTORY

- Who made the change?
- What changes have been made?
- When were the changes made?
- Why were the changes made?

EXHIBIT 42

OWNER AND AUTHOR IDENTIFICATION

- Who created the module?
- Who owns the module today?
- Who authored this particular change?

EXHIBIT 43

DATE/TIME STAMPS

- Each revision has one (SCM is time critical and time dependent).
- The archive file has its own.
- Revision creation date is restored upon retrieval.
- The stamp is used in the build process.

EXHIBIT 44

DATE/TIME STAMPS AND THE BUILD PROCESS

All file types:
- Executable; object; source; includes . . .

Dependencies:
- Executable $\Rightarrow$ object
- Object $\Rightarrow$ source
- Source $\Rightarrow$ include

Dates compared:
- Out-of-date $\Rightarrow$ rebuild
- Up-to-date $\Rightarrow$ no operation

EXHIBIT 45

THE CHANGE CONTROL BOARD (CCB)

The CCB is the critical link which will either allow changes to be managed or will cause the worst kinds of confusion. It always consists of at least:

1. Representative of users/client.
2. Head of 'engineering'.
   On small projects, lead programmer may be enough.
3. Representative of management.
4. QA.
   On small projects, the latter two are the same.

EXHIBIT 46

CCB FUNCTIONING

1. Define the information needs of the CCB.
2. Define how reused (or reusable) S/W should be affected by a change.
3. Do security questions affect your process of change?
4. How are source items associated with one another and with derived object items?

EXHIBIT 47

_____

RESOURCE ALLOCATION

Decisions affecting resource allocation and scheduling should be separated from those motivated by technical and/or marketing issues.
   Only then, justify and present them to management!

_____

EXHIBIT 48

_____

PR vs. CR

1. A 'Problem Report' (PR) is a type of change request (CR).
2. In very formal systems, a PR may cause a CR to be generated.
3. PR handling must be more careful than that of typical CRs because it is a difficulty which has already been discovered, and caused someone discomfort.

_____

EXHIBIT 49

_____

SOFTWARE PROBLEM REPORT PROCESSING

The discoverer of a problem writes an SPR.
   'Customer Service Department' validates the report.
   If the report is valid and the problem can be recreated (otherwise, close SPR):
- SPR is passed to the CCB for verification and technical impact
- If the SPR is processable:
  - Originator is notified of status
  - Engineering reanalyses for processing
  - If engineering agrees, scheduled for action (with CCB)
  - Problem is fixed (CM, test, . . .)
- originator is notified

Close SPR
Notify originator

_____

EXHIBIT 50

CHANGE IS OUR LIFE!

The software industry is driven by our ability to make changes to software (the 'soft').
Clearly, this is a critical activity.
It is very seldom performed well.
The activity consists of three classes of report:

- Errors/anomalies discovered
- Problems encountered
- Suggestions for changes/improvements

EXHIBIT 51

SUPPORT SOFTWARE

Describe what controls will be used to manage deliverable and non-deliverable items. Hardware CM is oriented towards deliverable items only.

EXHIBIT 52

STATUS ACCOUNTING ASKS:

- What happened?
- When did it happen?
- What were the reasons for the change?
- Who authorized the change?

EXHIBIT 53

ISSUES:

1. Acquire and maintain all information pertinent to the status of the project and its parts.
2. Report this to all levels of authority with a need to know.
3. Time is always a critical part of the status.
4. For each subsystem a separate account is maintained and transactions are recorded.
5. Typically a central journal logs activity and reports can be created from it.

EXHIBIT 54

NEVER EXPECT ALL REPORTS TO BE DETERMINABLE IN ADVANCE!

Minimal list of reports
- Transaction log
- Change log
- Item 'delta' report
- Resource usage
- 'Stock status' (status of items/named agglomerates)
- Changes in progress
- Deviations agreed upon

(This is still a wish list. No commercial system actually has them all.)

Points to be aware of:
1. How much formality is required by the customer (even if internal)?
2. Determine the audience of each report.
3. Project standards should be subordinate to corporate standards.

Typical ad hoc reports
- Problems in release ...
- Units delivered in time period ... to ...
- Changes resulting from problem ...
- Units to have been changed by change no. ...

EXHIBIT 55

ANSWERS TO BE EXPECTED FROM YOUR AUTOMATED SCM SYSTEM

- Audit trail of all activity
- File revision history
- Parallel lines of development
- Rebuilds of older version in the *exact* image of what they were
- Traceability
- Quality assurance support
- Project management documentation

EXHIBIT 56

THE REVISION MANAGER

- Restrict activities by user or group (access control)
- Merge concurrent changes
- Reduce storage requirements: no multiple copies, efficient delta storage
- Multi-dimensional delta reports
- Maintain journal of all activities
- Sophisticated report generation
- Compatible with multiple environments and platforms

EXHIBIT 57

THE BUILD MANAGER

- Compatible with project hierarchy
- Utilize file dependencies, relationships and date/time stamps
- Integrated with revision manager
- Ability to perform partial or full builds
- The specification language must be rich and expressive but upwards compatible from industry standards
- Compatible with multiple environments and platforms

EXHIBIT 58

AUDITS AND REVIEWS

- It is necessary to audit functional capabilities and physical parts of a system
- The audit is performed by management
  - Management auditors
  - Quality Assurance

Customers may need to be part of this process

EXHIBIT 59

AUDITS ARE ALWAYS APPLIED TO SUBCONTRACTORS!

EXHIBIT 60

AUDIT CRITERIA:

- Every major baseline/release must be audited
- For 'in-house' systems an informal audit is usually sufficient
- Periodic reviews must be held to determine progress
- Change control is the most important thing to audit!

EXHIBIT 61

AUDIT TRAIL

1. Provide project trace
2. Provide executable footprint
3. All modifications to any archive are reported
4. Log files may be:
   - Universal log (all activity)
   - Individual or multiple project logs
   - 'Functional area' logs

EXHIBIT 62

AUDIT TRAIL INFORMATION

- Who issued the command
- The command issued
- Which archive file(s) have been processed
- What actions have occurred as a result of the command
- What libraries are affected

EXHIBIT 63

WHO AUDITS?

- Configuration auditing is best performed by an external auditor.
  Why?
  Because a very high degree of objectivity is required when auditing a critical management function.
- The more sensitive the system is, the more this independence is critical.

EXHIBIT 64

US DOD-STD-2167/2168

Defines:
- Physical configuration audit (PCA)
- Functional configuration audit (FCA)

- PCA means all contracted-for items are present.
- FCA means someone acknowledges having tested against requirements.

EXHIBIT 65

IEEE/ANSI

The IEEE Standard documents for Software Configuration Management:

1. 'IEEE Standard for Software Configuration Management Plans'
   IEEE Std-828-1983
   IEEE Std-828-1990
2. 'IEEE Standard for Software Reviews and Audits'
   IEEE Std-1028-1988
3. 'IEEE Guide to Software Configuration Management'
   ANSI/IEEE Std-1042-1987

EXHIBIT 66

TOOLS, TECHNIQUES AND METHODOLOGIES

Minimal
- Database manager
- Report generator
- File system for check-in/check-out of subsystems
- Source code control
- Tool for baseline generation/regeneration
- Comparators
- File locking and security

Advanced
- Change request tracking
- Advanced access control
- 'Open' environment
- Cross-platform operational
- Object code storage
- Full project/directory tree transversal

EXHIBIT 67

TOOL IMPLEMENTATION STRATEGIES

Forward delta   vs.   Reverse delta storage
Massive database   vs.   Individual archives
Command line   vs.   GUI

EXHIBIT 68

FORWARD DELTA

- Maintains complete copy of original file
- Delta information appended to the file
- Latest revision must be computed
- Update requires computation of latest revision prior to generation of deltas for new revision
- More revisions only increase the retrieval time

EXHIBIT 69

REVERSE DELTA STORAGE

- Latest revision always immediately available
- Delta information stored for previous revisions
- Faster updates
- Latest revision the most frequently accessed
- No computation required for latest revision
- Efficient file storage

EXHIBIT 70

SUPPLIER CONTROL

- Items or subsystems which are subcontractor or vendor supplied must always be controlled and audited.
- The main contractor must be the one to determine the SCM procedures for all suppliers.

EXHIBIT 71

RECORDS RETENTION

1. Determine what change history needs to be retained and for how long.
2. How is the information to be stored and accessed?
3. Do different clients (of the system) have different configurations?
4. Must records of this be retained?

EXHIBIT 72

SOFTWARE LIFE-CYCLE

Design phase
- Design documents tracked with the SCM system: functional specifications; interface specifications; pseudo code.
- Create empty archive files with names and descriptions at the beginning of the project; fill them as the project progresses.

Implementation phase
1. Code generation: initial and intermediate revisions archived in predefined areas (directories)
2. Fine tune for: system architecture; functional specifications; interface specifications and user documentation

Testing phase
1. System integration by parts added together or via staged prototyping
2. Probably several versions created
3. Documentation types: user, maintenance, training
4. System debugging of design and code flaws

Beta phase
Bug Reports/Bug Fixes
- Internal/external
- Logic/design/code anomalies
- Documentation errors

Release phase
- Code and documentation finalized
- Final quality control procedures
- Shipments begin

Maintenance phase
1. Emergency bug fixes probably represent the greatest quantity of activity
2. Standard maintenance tasks
3. Bug reports/bug fixes:
   - internal/external
   - logic/design/code anomalies
   - documentation
4. New releases must be totally controlled

EXHIBIT 73

ABBREVIATIONS

CA	Configuration audit
CC	Configuration control
CCB	Change Control Board
CI	Configuration identification
CM	Configuration Management
CPCI	Computer program configuration item
SCM	Software Configuration Management
SCMP	Software Configuration Management Plan

EXHIBIT 74

TERMINOLOGY

Revision	An instance of a module or item
Version	An instance of a system
Variation	An alternate instance of development
Trunk	Primary development path
Branch	Variant development path
Workfile	A copy of the module for editing or viewing
Archive	The file used for storing the workfile with delta, revision and management information
Item	A unique object, to be identified and managed